THE VEGETARIAN YEAR

First published in Great Britain in 2015 by
Modern Books, an imprint of Elwin Street Limited
3 Percy Street
London W1T 1DE
www.elwinstreet.com

ISBN 978-1-9067-6-1509

67891054321

Printed in Malaysia

Approved by the Vegetarian Society

THE VEGETARIAN YEAR

365 days of healthy, seasonal recipes

Jane Hughes

Foreword by Rose Elliot

modern books

Contents

Foreword

Rose Elliot, Britain's foremost vegetarian cookery writer

I have known Jane Hughes for many years, as a writer, editor and tutor for the Vegetarian Society's Cordon Vert cookery school, and I am so happy that she has put her mouth-watering ideas and delectable recipes into this beautiful book. I feel sure it will appeal to vegetarians and vegans as well as to anyone who wants to increase the variety, interest and nutritional value of their meals by including more healthy, seasonal fruits and vegetables.

We all know that there are many excellent reasons to eat less meat and fish, and to include more fresh fruit and vegetables in our diet: to improve our health, to benefit the environment, to enjoy crops when they are at their peak and to save money; and now, Jane makes this simple for us to do by giving us 365 easy, tasty and colourful recipes in *The Vegetarian Year*.

I love the idea behind this book: to include one meal or dish that is seasonal and made from fresh natural produce every day of the year. What a great plan, especially when there are so many tempting recipes to choose from. Your 'dish of the day' could be a warming soup; a refreshing salad, starter or side dish; a filling and satisfying main; or even an indulgent pudding!

So go on, take the 365 challenge – eat a dish of seasonal fruits and vegetables every day for a year and see just how great that makes you feel.

The Versatility of Vegetables

This collection of 365 recipes offers something fresh, healthy and interesting for every single day of the year, making use of the fresh fruit, vegetables and herbs that are in season and responding to natural patterns, with hearty dishes in winter, and light meals in the spring and summer. Recipes are grouped into seasonal sections, and within the sections they follow a sequence: soups, salads and starters; main and side dishes; drinks and sweets. There are handy lists of the recipes at the beginning of each section, along with tips about which vegetables are available in each season of the year, and how to use them best.

As the seasons change, I hope you will enjoy browsing through each section of the book, reminding yourself of the ingredients that are at their freshest and most abundant, and savouring some classic flavour combinations – aromatic parsley and lemon with baby vegetables in spring; sweet, ripe tomatoes with gorgeous torn basil leaves in the summer; silky smooth squash soups with cinnamon and nutmeg in the autumn; hearty bean stews with a spicy chilli kick in the wintertime. You'll find plenty of inspiration, whether you're looking for new variations on old favourites, or dishes you've never tried before. And of course, don't be afraid to mix and match – if you're in the mood for a lemon tart, whether it's spring, summer, autumn or winter, go for it, and enjoy the time you spend in the kitchen.

Cook's Notes

Most of the following 365 recipes are suitable for beginners. Others provide a little more of a challenge, but none of the techniques are too difficult for an enthusiastic home cook. No special equipment is needed, but an inexpensive food processor will be invaluable for creating smooth soups, making breadcrumbs, chopping nuts and blending chopped herbs into curry pastes, pestos and sauces.

When cooking vegetarian and vegan foods, there are one or two things it's useful to know – for example, that many shop-bought desserts contain gelatin, which is an animal product, and that sometimes vegetable soups served in restaurants are made with meat-based stock. It's good to make your own so that you know exactly what you are eating! Some cheeses are also not suitable for vegetarians because they are made with animal rennet, so be sure to check the label. I buy free range eggs for all my recipes, and look for organic, non-GMO produce too.

Vegans don't consume any products that are derived from animals, including all dairy products, eggs and honey. Vegan recipes in this book are marked with a special logo. In many cases, it is also possible to 'veganise' the vegetarian recipes in this book by substituting vegan cheeses and non-dairy milks made with soya beans, almonds or oats.

When creating a vegan recipe, remember that vegetable stocks sometimes contain dairy products, pasta (especially fresh pasta) may contain eggs and not all margarines are completely free from animal products – look for brands that are marked suitable for vegans.

 Look out for this symbol when planning vegan meals.

Spring

Soups, salads and starters

Mains and sides

Drinks and sweets

Fresh in Season ...

Broad beans

Often the first fresh vegetable to be harvested in the spring, baby broad beans can be eaten in the pod. Later in the season, pod them and blanch them in boiling water, then rub off the greyish skins.

Rocket

Quick and easy to grow, rocket is generally used as a salad leaf, but its distinctive peppery flavour makes it a good choice for springtime soups and fresh pesto sauces to serve with pasta.

Asparagus

Choose slender stems with tight buds. A traditional asparagus steamer allows you to stand the spears upright in just a little water. This technique makes the stems tender without getting the delicate tips soggy.

Artichokes

Look for firm, medium-sized heads and leaves that are crisp. You will be discarding all but the heart and the most tender inner leaves, but the outer appearance gives good clues about the size and freshness of the centre.

Peas

Sweet and tender peas can be eaten raw, straight from the pod, or cooked for just a couple of minutes in boiling salted water. Unblemished pods can be used to make pea pod soup or even a traditional country wine.

Broccoli

Choose large, dense heads with no sign of yellowing, and use them soon after buying, as they don't keep well. The stems are edible – peel them with a potato peeler, cut into matchsticks or slices and add to a stir-fry.

Watercress

The peppery flavour of watercress makes it a welcome addition to the seasonal salad bowl. Try it in chilled soups, or use it in place of spinach to make pâtés or spanakopitta, a Greek-style dish with salty feta cheese encased in crisp filo pastry.

Baby vegetables

The earliest little carrots, courgettes and leeks look very pretty served whole as crudités. Steam them gently to serve hot on top of a bowl of pasta or rice. The season's freshest herbs are ideal partners for baby vegetables.

1 Chilli and coriander cakes

Makes 8

Ingredients

- 450 g potatoes
- 1 medium egg
- 6 spring onions
- 1 red chilli
- 55 g Cheddar cheese
- Handful fresh coriander
- Zest 1 lime
- 85 g Japanese panko breadcrumbs
- 2 tablespoons rapeseed oil

Preparation

Peel the potatoes and boil them in salted water until soft. Drain and set aside to dry out a little. Separate the egg into white and yolk. Trim and finely chop the spring onions. De-seed and finely chop the chilli. Grate the cheese. Chop the coriander.

Mash the potatoes with the egg yolk, spring onions, lime zest, chopped chilli, cheese and coriander.

Preheat the oven to 200°C. Beat the egg white a little and put it into a saucer. Put the breadcrumbs onto a plate.

Shape the mashed potato into small flattened cakes, and dip first in the egg white and then in the breadcrumbs. Place on a lightly greased baking tray and drizzle with the rapeseed oil. Bake for 20 minutes until crisp and golden.

2 Garlic, pea and broad bean dip

Serves 4

Ingredients

- 280 g fresh peas
- 280 g fresh broad beans
- 4 tablespoons olive oil
- 2 cloves garlic
- 1 lemon
- Salt and freshly ground black pepper

Preparation

Bring a large pan of salted water to the boil, add the peas and beans and cook for three minutes. Drain and refresh under cold water. Warm the olive oil in a frying pan. Peel and chop the garlic and fry it very gently for three minutes. Zest the lemon and squeeze out the juice.

Put the peas and beans into a food processor with the garlic and the olive oil, the lemon zest and lemon juice. Blend to a purée and season well to taste. Serve as a dip, or spread onto toasted ciabatta slices.

3 Roasted red pepper and tomato soup

Serves 4

Ingredients

* 2 red peppers
* 1 onion
* 450 g tomatoes
* 3 tablespoons olive oil
* 1 tablespoon balsamic vinegar
* 300 ml milk
* ½ teaspoon brown sugar

Preparation

Preheat the oven to 190°C. Cut the peppers into quarters and discard the seeds and white pith. Peel the onion and chop into quarters. Cut the tomatoes in half. Put the vegetables in a large mixing bowl and stir in the olive oil and vinegar, making sure that all the pieces are well covered. Transfer the vegetables to a baking tray and roast for 30 minutes, until beginning to brown.

Allow the vegetables to cool, then blend in a blender, adding sufficient water to make a thick purée. Transfer the mixture to a saucepan and stir in the milk and the sugar. Warm through and add more water if necessary to achieve your ideal consistency.

Many roasted vegetables can be made into soup this way. If you are using the oven for a different recipe, consider roasting some vegetables at the same time. Store the vegetables in the refrigerator, and you can make a delicious soup in minutes!

4 Edamame fritters with wasabi

Serves 4

Ingredients

* 2 medium eggs
* 1 teaspoon wasabi powder
* 2 cloves garlic
* 2.5 cm ginger root
* 115 g plain flour
* Sea salt
* 450 g fresh or frozen edamame beans
* Vegetable oil for frying

Preparation

Beat the eggs. Mix the wasabi powder with a little water to make a paste. Peel and crush the garlic. Grate the ginger, then gather up the pieces and squeeze them over a small bowl to collect the juice. Discard the pulp.

Put the flour and a pinch of salt into a large bowl, and beat in the eggs, wasabi paste, garlic and ginger juice. Mix the edamame beans thoroughly into the batter.

Pour the oil into a deep frying pan, to a depth of around 1 cm. Heat the oil until a little batter dropped into it sizzles straight away. Gently fry small spoonfuls of the edamame mixture, until crisp and golden on both sides.

Edamame are fresh green soya beans, popped out of their pods. Rich in protein, they make a great addition to salads.

5 Crudités with sherry vinaigrette

Serves 4

Ingredients

- 600 g mixed fresh, colourful baby vegetables: carrots, radishes, asparagus spears, baby fennel

For the dressing

- 1 shallot
- 6 tablespoons extra-virgin olive oil
- 2 tablespoons sherry vinegar
- 1 teaspoon Dijon mustard
- ½ teaspoon coarse-ground salt

Preparation

Make the dressing first. Peel the shallot and chop it as finely as you can. Mix it with the oil and vinegar, mustard and salt.

Trim and rinse the vegetables – it should not be necessary to peel them. Cut any that are large into bite-sized pieces.

In a large bowl, mix the vegetables with the dressing, cover and chill for at least three hours – overnight is fine. Toss again before serving.

This classic French vinaigrette brings out the flavour of each vegetable without the need for any further dips.

6 Tomato and basil bruschetta

Serves 4

Ingredients

- 1 small French baguette or similar style Italian bread
- 600 g ripe tomatoes
- 85 g black pitted olives
- 2 cloves garlic
- Few sprigs fresh basil
- 1 tablespoon olive oil, plus extra to serve
- 1 teaspoon balsamic vinegar
- Few fresh chives
- Salt and freshly ground black pepper

Preparation

Slice the bread and toast it lightly on both sides. Roughly chop the tomatoes, slice the olives and peel and crush the garlic. Strip the basil leaves from their stalks and tear roughly. Mix the tomatoes, olives and garlic together in a large bowl with the basil, olive oil and balsamic vinegar.

Top each slice of bread with a generous spoonful of the tomato mixture. Trim and chop the chives into 2.5-cm pieces, or leave whole, to garnish. Finish the dish with freshly ground salt and black pepper, and an extra drizzle of olive oil.

7 Miso and soba soup

Serves 4

Ingredients

- 85 g dried soba noodles
- 55 g firm tofu
- 3 spring onions
- Handful fresh coriander
- 3 tablespoons miso paste
- Pinch red pepper flakes

Preparation

Bring a large saucepan of salted water to the boil and cook the noodles for up to eight minutes, until tender. Drain and refresh under cold running water.

Drain and press the tofu, and cut into small cubes. Trim and chop the spring onions. Finely chop the coriander.

In a separate, large saucepan, bring 1 litre of water to the boil. Remove from the heat. Put the miso into a small bowl or cup and stir in a little of the hot water to make a runny paste. Stir this back into the pan of hot water, tasting after each addition, until the strength suits your taste. Stir in the tofu.

Divide the cooked noodles between two to four serving bowls, cover with the soup and top with the chopped onions, coriander and red pepper flakes.

In Japanese, the word soba is synonymous with both the grain buckwheat and these buckwheat noodles. The noodles are thin (unlike the thicker udon noodles) and are often served in soups or chilled with a dipping sauce. By not boiling this nutritious soup after adding the miso, you will preserve more of the valuable B vitamins that it contains.

8 Quick minestrone

Serves 4

Ingredients

- 1 onion
- 2 carrots
- 2 potatoes
- 2 leeks
- 2 sticks celery
- 250 g green beans
- 500 g tomatoes
- 350 g courgettes
- 100 g dried pasta: penne or fusilli
- Large sprig fresh rosemary
- 1 x 400 g can of red kidney beans
- Salt and freshly ground black pepper

Preparation

Peel the onion, carrots and potatoes, and trim the leeks and celery sticks. Finely chop them all and place in a large saucepan with 2.5 litres boiling water. Simmer for 10 minutes.

Trim and chop the green beans, and chop the tomatoes. Trim and dice the courgettes. Add these vegetables to the pot along with the pasta, rosemary and drained, rinsed kidney beans. Season with salt and pepper and cook until the pasta is cooked through.

9 Essential lemon oil

Serves 4

Ingredients
- 2 unwaxed lemons
- 225 ml olive oil

Preparation
Zest the lemons. Place the zest with the oil in a small saucepan and warm gently for three minutes. Remove from the heat and leave to cool. Transfer to a bowl, cover and infuse for 24 hours. Strain the oil into a sterilised bottle and store in the refrigerator for up to a month.

Olive oil begins to solidify when it is stored in the refrigerator, so you will need to allow it to come to room temperature before you can drizzle it over some freshly steamed asparagus spears.

10 Herbal vinegar

Serves 4

Ingredients
- Fresh herbs of your choice: basil, lemon balm, rosemary, mint, oregano and bay leaves are all good
- Sufficient white wine vinegar or cider vinegar to fill your chosen bottle(s)

Preparation
Wash and dry the fresh herbs gently to avoid bruising them, and pack them into a sterilised jar. Fill the jar with vinegar, seal and store in a dark place at room temperature. Leave for between three and six weeks, depending on how strong you want the taste to be.

Strain the vinegar through a muslin cloth and transfer to a freshly sterilised bottle. Add one or two fresh sprigs of one of your chosen herbs before sealing.

11 Red pepper caponata with green olives

Serves 4

Ingredients
- 8 red peppers
- 6 tablespoons extra-virgin olive oil
- 175 g pickled silverskin onions
- 175 g green olives
- Salt and freshly ground black pepper
- Handful fresh parsley

Preparation
De-seed the peppers and thinly slice. Warm the olive oil in a pan, add the peppers and mix well so that they are covered in oil. Cover the pan and turn the heat to the lowest possible setting. Cook for 20 minutes, stirring occasionally.

Slice away and discard the bases of the onions. Put the onions into a large bowl of boiling water. Leave for three minutes, before scooping out with a slotted spoon. The onions should separate easily into individual 'leaves'.

Arrange the warm peppers and oil on a serving dish, with the onion pieces and green olives on top. Season generously with salt and pepper. Chop the fresh parsley and sprinkle over the warm caponata before serving.

Caponata originated as a Sicilian salad made from cooked aubergine and capers, but the term has come to be used for all sorts of warm or chilled salads made with soft-cooked Mediterranean-style vegetables.

12 Warm rocket, mushroom and sugar snap pea salad

Serves 4

Ingredients

- 225 g suger snap peas
- 225 g red pepper
- 225 g rocket
- 450 g mushrooms
- 25 g salted butter

For the dressing

- 2.5 cm ginger root
- Sprig fresh thyme
- 3 tablespoons cider vinegar
- 90 ml olive oil
- 1 clove garlic

Preparation

Start by making the dressing. Grate the ginger and then squeeze out the juice. Discard the pulp. Strip the thyme leaves from their stalks and chop. Put the olive oil, cider vinegar, ginger juice, thyme and garlic in a blender or food processor and process until smooth.

Steam the sugar snap peas for three minutes – they should be bright green and still quite crisp. Refresh them under cold running water. De-seed and roughly chop the red pepper. Place in a large mixing bowl with the sugar snap peas. Roughly chop the rocket and add to the bowl.

Wipe and slice the mushrooms. Melt the butter in a frying pan and fry the mushrooms gently for about eight minutes. Stir the warm mushrooms into the salad. Toss the dressing through the vegetables and serve immediately.

This salad is best eaten when the mushrooms are still warm. The butter they are cooked in can go into the salad, too.

13 Rhubarb, pecan and goat's cheese salad

Serves 4

Ingredients

- 3 sticks rhubarb
- 2 tablespoons sugar
- 55 g pecans
- 175 g mixed salad
- 55 g goat's cheese

For the dressing

- 1 shallot
- 2 tablespoons balsamic vinegar
- 1 tablespoon rapeseed oil
- Salt and freshly ground black pepper

Preparation

Preheat the oven to 230°C.

Trim the rhubarb and cut into 1-cm chunks. Place in a mixing bowl and toss with the sugar. Transfer to a baking tray lined with baking parchment and bake for five minutes, until just starting to soften.

Roughly chop the pecans. Toast them in a dry, heavy frying pan for a few minutes, until aromatic and beginning to brown.

To make the dressing, peel the shallot and chop it very finely. Beat with the remaining dressing ingredients.

Toss the dressing through the salad and arrange on a large serving plate topped with the rhubarb, crumbled cheese and nuts.

14 Avocado and farfalle salad with mint

Serves 4

Ingredients

- 250 g dried pasta: farfalle or fusilli work well
- 2 ripe avocados
- 1 lime
- Handful fresh mint
- 1 red chilli
- 2 tablespoons olive oil
- Salt and freshly ground black pepper

Preparation

Bring a large saucepan of salted water to the boil and cook the pasta until just tender. Refresh under cold running water and set to one side.

Peel and stone the avocados. Zest and juice the lime. Finely chop the mint. De-seed and finely chop the chilli. Reserve half an avocado, and mash the rest together with the lime juice and zest, mint, chilli, olive oil and seasoning. Dice or slice the reserved avocado half.

Toss the avocado mixture through the pasta and serve immediately, topped with the reserved avocado pieces.

15 Chickpea and grape salad with citrus dressing

Serves 4

Ingredients
- 350 g sprouted chickpeas
- 350 g seedless grapes
- Handful fresh parsley
- ½ teaspoon fennel seeds
- 55 g sunflower seeds

For the dressing
- 1 orange
- 1 lemon
- 2 teaspoons Dijon mustard
- 2 tablespoons flaxseed oil
- 2 teaspoons cider vinegar
- Freshly ground black pepper

Preparation
Make the dressing first. Cut the orange and lemon in half and remove the seeds. Chop them into smaller pieces, keeping the skins on. Purée in a blender with the remaining dressing ingredients, adding a little extra water or orange juice if necessary, to make a pourable dressing.

Rinse the sprouted chickpeas and cut the grapes in half. Finely chop the parsley. Transfer the salad ingredients to a large bowl and toss the dressing through immediately before serving.

16 Blue cheese and walnut salad

Serves 4

Ingredients
- 225 g mixed salad
- 100 g walnut pieces
- 100 g vegetarian blue cheese
- 3 tablespoons walnut oil
- 2 tablespoons cider vinegar

Preparation
Divide the salad between four serving plates and top with the walnuts and crumbled cheese. Beat the oil and vinegar together and serve separately so that guests can dress their own salad.

Not all blue cheeses are suitable for vegetarians – Gorgonzola, for example, is made with animal rennet. Be sure to read the label before you buy.

17 Superfood salad

Serves 4

Ingredients
- 25 g quinoa
- 200 g broccoli
- 115 g cucumber
- 1 lemon
- Handful fresh, flat-leaf parsley
- Handful fresh mint
- 1 avocado
- 25 g alfalfa sprouts
- 3 tablespoons olive oil
- 115 g feta cheese
- 1 tablespoon pumpkin seeds
- Pinch sumac
- Salt and freshly ground black pepper

Preparation
Bring a pan of salted water to the boil. Cook the quinoa for up to 15 minutes, until tender. Drain and spread on a plate to cool.

Chop the broccoli into bite-sized pieces. Chop the cucumber into batons. Zest and juice the lemon. Roughly chop the herbs. Just before you are ready to serve the salad, peel and chop the avocado – it will begin to brown if you prepare it too early.

Transfer the quinoa into a large mixing bowl and stir in the broccoli, cucumber, avocado, alfalfa sprouts and chopped herbs. Add the lemon zest and juice and the olive oil, and toss together. Top each portion of the salad with crumbled feta cheese, pumpkin seeds, a dusting of sumac and salt and pepper.

18 Ginger and sesame wakame salad

Serves 4

Ingredients
- 25 g dried wakame
- 1 clove garlic
- 1 cm ginger root
- ½ red chilli
- 2 tablespoons soy sauce
- 2 tablespoons honey
- 1 tablespoon lemon juice
- 1 teaspoon toasted sesame oil

Preparation
Soak the wakame in cold water for an hour, then drain and finely shred. Peel and crush the garlic. Peel the ginger and chop finely. De-seed the chilli and chop finely.

Mix all the ingredients thoroughly and chill for an hour before serving.

Wakame is a Japanese seaweed with a subtle, sweet taste. It is sold dried, and can be crumbled over foods or rehydrated and added to salads

19 Spicy marinated daikon salad

Serves 4

Ingredients
- 400 g daikon
  (Japanese white radish)
- 1 red pepper
- 2 spring onions
- 1 date

For the dressing
- ½ red chilli
- 1 clove garlic
- 1 cm ginger root
- 1 tablespoon soy sauce
- 2 tablespoons cider vinegar
- 2 teaspoons honey
- 1 tablespoon toasted sesame oil

Preparation
Peel the daikon and chop it into matchsticks. Finely dice the red pepper, and trim and chop the spring onions. Finely chop the date. Place these ingredients in a large bowl.

To make the dressing, de-seed the red chilli and chop it very finely. Peel and crush the garlic. Peel the ginger and chop it very finely. Combine with the remaining dressing ingredients, adding a little cold water to achieve the desired consistency.

Toss the dressing through the salad and chill for an hour before serving.

Top each portion with a little finely grated red cabbage or carrot to add a splash of colour to this refreshing salad.

20 Blueberry, blue cheese and watercress salad

Serves 4

Ingredients
- 85 g watercress
- 85 g baby spinach
- 115 g blueberries
- 85 g vegetarian blue cheese

For the dressing
- 115 g blueberries
- 1 tablespoon balsamic vinegar
- 1 tablespoon honey
- 3 tablespoons olive oil

Preparation
Make the dressing first. Place all the ingredients in a blender or food processor and blend until smooth.

Wash and roughly chop the watercress and spinach. Place in a large bowl. Toss the blueberries and the dressing through the salad. Transfer the salad to a large serving plate, top with crumbled blue cheese and serve immediately.

21 Vegetable tempura with citrus dipping sauce

Serves 4

Ingredients
- 2 red peppers
- 1 green pepper
- 2 small onions
- 6 spring onions
- Vegetable oil for deep-frying

For the batter
- 10 g plain flour
- 1 tablespoon cornflour
- 125 ml sparkling mineral water
- Pinch salt

For the dipping sauce
- 3 tablespoons soy sauce
- 3 tablespoons mirin (Japanese rice wine)
- Juice 1 orange
- 1 teaspoon sugar

Preparation

Beat all the batter ingredients together to make a smooth, thin batter. Make the dipping sauce by mixing all the ingredients together in a small bowl and stirring until the sugar is dissolved.

De-seed the peppers and cut into bite-sized pieces. Peel and slice the onions into rings. Trim the spring onions.

Heat the oil in a large pan or large wok. Dip the prepared vegetables into the batter and fry in small batches – don't overload the pan as this will lower the temperature of the oil and make your tempura soggy. Drain on kitchen towel and serve immediately with the dipping sauce.

This dish is best served as a starter, snack or side dish rather than the centrepiece of a meal. You can also use vegetables such as courgettes, carrots or broccoli here – just chop into small pieces first.

22 Fattoush salad

Serves 4

Ingredients

- 500 g broad beans
- 1 cucumber
- Small bunches of fresh mint, parsley and chives
- 2 wholewheat pitta breads
- 1 lemon
- 4 tablespoons olive oil
- 1 teaspoon honey (plus extra to garnish)
- 100 g feta cheese
- Freshly ground black pepper

Preparation

Bring a large pan of salted water to the boil and cook the beans for three minutes. Drain and refresh under cold water, then pop the bright green beans out of their grey-green skins and discard the skins.

Trim and chop the cucumber, and finely chop the herbs. Toast the pitta breads and then tear them into bite-sized pieces. Zest and juice the lemon, and whisk the zest and juice together with the olive oil and honey.

Transfer all the prepared ingredients to a large mixing bowl, toss together gently and top with crumbled feta cheese, freshly ground black pepper and a final drizzle of honey.

Fattoush is a traditional bread salad from the Middle East. Broad beans provide another texture and a little extra goodness!

23 Layered beetroot salad

Serves 4

Ingredients

- 3 beetroots
- 3 carrots
- 1 small red cabbage
- ½ red onion
- 2 tablespoons olive oil
- 2 tablespoons balsamic vinegar

Preparation

Peel the beetroots and carrots, and trim the outer leaves and core of the cabbage. Grate them all separately. Peel the onion and slice it as thinly as you can. Mix the oil and vinegar together to make the salad dressing.

To serve, layer the grated carrot, beetroots and cabbage into small glass bowls, or pile onto a large serving plate. You can mix them together, but it looks nicer if you keep each ingredient separate, and you can taste their individual flavours too. Garnish with the finely sliced red onions and the balsamic dressing.

If you can find golden beetroots or purple carrots, this is the perfect way to showcase their unusual colours.

24 Pea pakoras

Serves 4

Ingredients
- 500 g potatoes
- 225 g fresh or frozen peas
- 1 teaspoon ground coriander
- 1 teaspoon ground cumin
- ½ teaspoon chilli powder

Preparation
Preheat the oven to 200°C.

Peel the potatoes and cut them into small chunks. Heat a large pan of salted water and boil the potatoes for up to 15 minutes, until cooked through. Add the peas to cook in the same pan for the last five minutes. Use a slotted spoon to retrieve around half of the peas, and set these aside. Drain the remaining peas with the potatoes and mash them together with the ground coriander, cumin and chilli powder. Stir in the reserved whole peas.

Form the mixture into 16 to 20 small balls and put on a baking tray lined with baking parchment. Bake for 20 minutes, until crisp and golden.

Pakoras are fried savoury snacks, most commonly a mixture of vegetables dipped in a batter made with chickpea flour. Pakoras are thought to have originated in India but are popular across southern Asia.

25 Onion and potato bhajis
Makes 8

Ingredients
- 3 onions
- 1 potato
- Few sprigs fresh coriander
- 1 teaspoon garam masala
- 115 g gram (chickpea) flour
- Rapeseed oil, for frying

Preparation
Peel the onions and finely slice. Peel the potato and coarsely grate it. Chop the coriander. Mix the onion, potato, coriander, garam masala and gram flour together thoroughly to form a stiff dough.

Heat the oil in a frying pan and fry flattened teaspoons of the mixture gently on both sides for about eight minutes, until cooked through and crisp.

Bhajis are a popular street food in India. They are deep-fried snacks made from grated onion (or other vegetables) mixed with a batter made from chickpea flour.

26 Cashew nut croquettes

Makes 12

Ingredients

- 1 medium egg
- 800 g potatoes
- 1 tablespoon salted butter
- Salt and freshly ground black pepper
- 140 g cashew nuts
- 25 g plain flour
- 2 tablespoons rapeseed oil

Preparation

Separate the egg into yolk and white.

Peel the potatoes and boil them in salted water for up to 20 minutes, until soft. Drain and mash them with the butter, seasoning and egg yolk. Leave to cool.

Put the cashews into a dry, heavy-bottomed saucepan and heat them gently, stirring frequently, until they begin to colour. Turn them onto a chopping board and, when cool enough, chop finely.

Beat the egg white lightly and put it into a saucer. Put the chopped nuts onto a plate.

Preheat the oven to 200°C. Working on a floured surface, roll the mashed potato into croquette shapes, ensure that they are coated with flour and then dip them into the egg white. Next, dip them into the chopped nuts and make sure the surfaces are covered. Put on a lightly greased baking tray.

When all the croquettes have been made, drizzle them with rapeseed oil and bake for 20 minutes, until golden.

27 Braised lettuce with creamy spring onion dip

Serves 4

Ingredients

- 2 Little Gem lettuces
- 1 bunch spring onions
- 25 g salted butter
- 2 tablespoons olive oil
- 2 teaspoons plain flour
- 275 ml vegetable stock
- 250 g fresh peas
- Salt and freshly ground black pepper
- Juice 1 lemon

For the dip

- 1 bunch spring onions
- 400 ml sour cream
- Salt and freshly ground black pepper

Preparation

Trim the lettuce stalks and slice the lettuce from base to tip, about 1-cm thick. Trim and finely chop the spring onions.

Melt the butter with the oil in a large saucepan. Stir in the flour, cook for a few seconds and then gradually add the vegetable stock, stirring constantly to prevent any lumps from forming.

Add the lettuce, peas and spring onions, season with a little salt and pepper and simmer, covered, for 10 minutes, until the vegetables are tender. Add the lemon juice just before serving.

To make the dip, trim the spring onions and chop very finely. Stir into the sour cream and season to taste with salt and pepper.

This simple dip is also perfect with fresh crudités.

28 Golden baby potatoes
Serves 4

Ingredients
- 500 g baby new potatoes
- 3 onions
- Few sprigs fresh thyme
- Small handful fresh parsley
- 25 g salted butter
- 2 bay leaves
- 2 tablespoons olive oil
- Salt and freshly ground black pepper

Preparation
Boil the new potatoes in salted water for about 25 minutes, until tender. Drain and set aside. Peel and finely slice the onions. Strip the thyme leaves from the stalks. Chop the parsley.

Melt the butter in a large saucepan and stir in the onions, thyme leaves and bay leaves. Cover, turn the heat to minimum and cook for up to 20 minutes, until the onions are very soft. Then turn up the heat and stir for a few more minutes, until golden.

Slice or halve the new potatoes and stir them into the onions along with the olive oil. Fry until golden, around 10 minutes. Stir the chopped parsley into the dish immediately before serving and season with salt and freshly ground black pepper.

29 Spring vegetables with red pesto
Serves 4

Ingredients
- 225 g new potatoes
- 225 g baby carrots
- 175 g baby courgettes
- 8 shallots
- 85 g baby asparagus spears
- 85 g fine green beans

For the pesto
- 2 tomatoes
- Handful fresh basil
- 2 cloves garlic
- 55 g vegetarian Parmesan-style cheese
- 1 tablespoon olive oil

Preparation
Bring a pan of salted water to the boil and cook the potatoes for up to 15 minutes, until tender. Trim the remaining vegetables and chop into bite-sized pieces, then steam them for 10 minutes, until just tender.

To make the pesto, roughly chop the tomatoes and basil. Peel and crush the garlic, and grate the cheese. Put all the ingredients into a food processor, and process to a rough paste.

Toss the cooked vegetables with the pesto and serve immediately.

30 Curried baby potatoes

Serves 4

Ingredients

- 350 g new potatoes
- 1 onion
- 2.5 cm ginger root
- 2 tablespoons vegetable oil
- ½ teaspoon turmeric
- ½ teaspoon cumin seeds
- ½ teaspoon cayenne pepper
- Juice ½ lemon
- Pinch salt
- 1 tablespoon fresh, chopped coriander

Preparation

Parboil the potatoes until they are not quite softened. Drain and cut into bite-sized pieces.

Peel and roughly chop the onion. Peel and grate the ginger. Warm the oil in a large frying pan and gently fry the onion and ginger for five minutes, until the onion is soft and translucent. Stir in the turmeric, cumin seeds and cayenne. Mix well, add the potatoes and cook, stirring constantly, for five more minutes. Stir in the lemon juice, salt and chopped fresh coriander and serve hot, as a side dish or wrapped in Crispy Chickpea Crêpes (see page 47).

31 Stir-fried baby vegetables with water chestnuts

Serves 4

Ingredients

- 900 g mixed fresh baby vegetables: carrots, spring onions, summer squash
- 1 onion
- 115 g water chestnuts
- 4 cloves garlic
- 4 cm ginger root
- 3 tablespoons toasted sesame oil
- 3 tablespoons soy sauce

Preparation

Trim and rinse the vegetables, and finely slice. Peel and slice the onion. Slice the water chestnuts. Peel the garlic and slice each clove from top to bottom to make as many thin slices as you can. Peel and grate the ginger.

Put the soy sauce and sesame oil into a large pan or wok and stir-fry all the ingredients together on a high heat, stirring constantly, for up to five minutes, until the vegetables are heated through but still crisp. Serve immediately.

32 Spring vegetables with orange and fennel seeds

Serves 4

Ingredients

- 450 g fresh mixed baby vegetables:
  carrots, fennel, pak choi, asparagus
- 1 orange
- 2 teaspoons fennel seeds
- 4 tablespoons extra-virgin olive oil
- Few sprigs fresh parsley

Preparation

Trim and rinse the vegetables – it should not be necessary
to peel them, and the carrots are attractive with some of
their greenery left intact. Cut any large vegetables into
crudité-sized sticks. Juice and zest the orange. Crush the
fennel seeds with a pestle and mortar or a rolling pin,
mix together with the olive oil, orange juice and orange
zest, and combine all the ingredients in a large bowl.
Chill for 20 minutes. Chop the fresh parsley and stir into
the vegetables before serving.

*Fennel seeds have a delicate aniseed flavour and are said to aid
digestion and settle the stomach. To ensure the fennel seeds
do not scatter when crushed with a rolling pin, cover them
with cling film.*

33 Gingered spring greens

Serves 4

Ingredients
- 450 g spring greens: chard, mustard greens, dandelion greens and kale are all good
- 2.5 cm ginger root
- 1 clove garlic
- 1 tablespoon olive oil
- 1 tablespoon cider vinegar
- 1 tablespoon soy sauce
- 2 tablespoons toasted sesame oil
- 1 tablespoon sesame seeds

Preparation
Wash the greens and discard any woody stems or discoloured leaves. Finely shred the greens. Peel and finely chop the ginger. Peel and crush the garlic.

In a large pan or wok, warm the olive oil and fry the ginger and garlic over a gentle heat for one minute, then stir in the vinegar and soy sauce. Raise the heat to medium and add the greens and 2 tablespoons of water. Cover and cook for five minutes, then remove the lid, toss the greens to ensure that they cook evenly and cook, uncovered, for a further three minutes until tender. Remove the pan or wok from the heat, and drain off any excess cooking liquid before serving.

Drizzle each portion with sesame oil and top with a sprinkling of sesame seeds.

34 Quinoa with currants and spicy onions

Serves 4

Ingredients
- 350 g quinoa
- 70 g currants
- 1 red onion
- 2 tablespoons olive oil
- ½ teaspoon cinnamon
- ½ teaspoon ground ginger
- ½ teaspoon ground coriander
- ½ teaspoon turmeric
- ½ teaspoon ground cumin
- 4 tablespoons toasted flaked almonds
- Handful fresh, flat-leaf parsley
- Handful fresh coriander

Preparation
Bring a saucepan of salted water to the boil and cook the quinoa and currants together for about 15 minutes, or until the quinoa is tender. Drain and set aside to cool slightly.

Peel and finely chop the onion. Warm the oil in a frying pan and fry the onion with the spices for five minutes, until the onion is very soft.

Transfer the quinoa to a large mixing bowl, fluff it up gently with a fork and fold in the cooked onions, almonds and herbs.

Five ways with broad beans

35

In their pods

Broad beans can only be eaten in their pods when they are very young, which makes them a real delicacy. Simply top and tail, and eat them raw with a dipping pot of olive oil and balsamic vinegar.

36

Shelled

Once shelled, broad beans have a bright green bean inside a grey-green individual skin. The skins are edible and can be left on for more substantial salads and sides. Boil for two minutes with some fresh peas, then toss with crisp fried onion and fresh herbs. Mint, sage, lemon thyme and basil are all good.

37

Double-shelled

This involves removing the grey-green outer skin that surrounds each bean. Plunge the beans into boiling water to loosen the skins, pop out the bright green beans and mix into a three-bean salad with kidney beans, chickpeas and a spicy vinaigrette.

38

Fried

Fry the beans with crushed garlic in a little olive oil or butter – they only need a few moments to warm through. Don't let the garlic brown or the taste will be bitter. Serve over a heap of hot mashed potatoes.

39

Puréed

Blitz leftover beans from the recipes above in a food processor and season generously to make a dip or a flavoursome sandwich filling.

40 Courgette and broccoli tagliatelle

Serves 4

Ingredients

- 2 courgettes
- 225 g tenderstem broccoli
- 1 yellow pepper
- 300 g dried tagliatelle
- Handful flat-leaf parsley
- 2 tablespoons olive oil
- Juice ½ lemon
- Salt and freshly ground black pepper

Preparation

Trim and slice the courgettes into sticks. Trim the broccoli, slicing through any thicker stems. De-seed and finely slice the pepper.

Cook the pasta in boiling water until tender. Steam the vegetables for 10 minutes, or until tender – you may be able to save energy by putting the steamer over the pasta pan.

Finely chop half of the parsley and leave the rest whole. Mix the oil, lemon juice and salt and pepper together. To serve, toss the pasta with the warm vegetables, chopped parsley and dressing. Garnish with the reserved parsley sprigs.

Tenderstem broccoli has longer, finer stalks than broccoli, so it is good to eat, but also looks very pretty on the plate. If you can only get curly parsley, use half the quantity and chop it finely. A mixture of green and white tagliatelle with yellow courgette looks attractive, but don't use black pasta as it is usually coloured with squid ink.

41 Stir-fried asparagus with dates and carrots

Serves 4

Ingredients

- 12 asparagus spears
- 2.5 cm ginger root
- 3 carrots
- 1 onion
- 6 dates
- 2 tablespoons olive oil
- 1 teaspoon sesame oil
- 4 star anise
- Freshly ground black pepper

Preparation

Trim the asparagus spears and cut any thick stems in half lengthways. Peel the ginger and chop finely. Peel the carrots and chop into thin matchsticks. Peel and slice the onion. Roughly chop the dates.

Warm the olive oil and sesame oil together in a large pan or wok. Add the star anise and ginger, and cook for a minute before stirring in the carrot and onion. Stir-fry for four minutes.

Add the asparagus, dates and black pepper and mix well. Stir in 2 tablespoons of water, cover and cook for five minutes, until the asparagus is tender.

42 Authentic falafel

Serves 4

Ingredients

- 600 g tinned chickpeas
- 1 onion
- 2 cloves garlic
- 115g bread
- Few sprigs fresh coriander
- 1 medium egg
- 55g fresh breadcrumbs
- ½ teaspoon dried red chilli flakes
- Salt and freshly ground black pepper
- Rapeseed oil, for frying

Preparation

Drain and rinse the chickpeas. Peel and finely chop the onion. Peel and crush the garlic. Tear the bread into pieces. Chop the coriander. Beat the egg and put the breadcrumbs onto a large flat plate.

Place the chickpeas, onion, garlic, torn bread, chilli flakes, egg, coriander and seasoning into the bowl of a food processor and process until smooth.

Divide the mixture into 12 portions. Shape them into patties and roll them in the breadcrumbs to coat them.

Heat the oil in a frying pan. Flatten the patties with the back of a spoon and fry gently on both sides for about eight minutes, until cooked through and crisp.

Serve these as they do in the Middle East – inside warmed flat breads such as pitta, with salad and tahini sauce or hummus.

43 Vegetable and almond paella

Serves 4

Ingredients

- 1 onion
- 1 clove garlic
- 225 g mixed spring vegetables: beans, peas, mangetout, baby courgettes, leeks, spring onions, baby carrots
- 1 green pepper
- 1 stick celery
- Sprig fresh tarragon
- 2 teaspoons rapeseed oil
- 85 g blanched almonds
- 175 g brown rice
- Pinch saffron strands

Preparation

Peel and finely chop the onion. Peel and crush the garlic. Chop all the remaining vegetables into bite-sized pieces. Chop the fresh tarragon.

Warm the oil in a large saucepan and fry the onion for three minutes, then add the garlic and cook gently for a further two minutes. Stir in the almonds and the rice, mix well and cook for a further two minutes, stirring constantly. Add the celery, green pepper, mixed vegetables and tarragon. Cook for a further five minutes.

Add 600 ml boiling water and the saffron strands. Bring to the boil, cover and simmer for 30 minutes, until the rice is cooked and the liquid has been absorbed.

You'll need a large, wide pan with a lid for this Spanish rice dish.

44 Tofu pad thai

Serves 4

Ingredients

- 400 g firm tofu
- 8 tablespoons soy sauce
- 225 g dried fine rice noodles
- 1 onion
- 4 cloves garlic
- 85 g peanuts
- 175 g beansprouts
- Juice 1 lemon
- ½ teaspoon sugar
- Red pepper flakes, to taste
- 2 tablespoons rapeseed oil

Preparation

Drain the tofu, cut it into bite-sized pieces and put it into a shallow dish with half the soy sauce. Leave to marinate for at least one hour, then gently cook in a dry frying pan, turning to seal each side.

Soak the noodles in cold water for 20 minutes. Drain through a colander.

Peel and finely chop the onion. Peel and chop the garlic. Roughly chop the peanuts.

Heat the oil in a wok and fry the onion and garlic for one minute, then stir in the tofu, noodles, beansprouts, peanuts, lemon juice, sugar, red pepper flakes and remaining soy sauce. Toss over a high heat for up to three minutes, until heated through.

45 Rice noodles with shallots and garlic

Serves 4

Ingredients

- 225 g dried fine rice noodles
- 4 shallots
- 4 cloves garlic
- ½ teaspoon sugar
- 1 tablespoon mirin (Japanese rice wine)
- 2 tablespoons soy sauce
- Freshly ground black pepper
- 2 tablespoons rapeseed oil

Preparation

Soak the noodles in cold water for 20 minutes, then transfer to a colander to drain. Peel and slice the shallots and the garlic. Mix the sugar, mirin and soy sauce together in a small bowl with 1 tablespoon of water.

Warm the oil in a wok and fry the shallots and garlic for a minute, stirring constantly. Add the soy sauce mixture and the noodles, and stir-fry for about three minutes, until the dish is heated through. Season with freshly ground black pepper.

Rice noodles are popular in the cuisine of Eastern and South-Eastern Asia and are generally only lightly cooked to retain a slightly chewy texture. However, all sorts of noodles are used in East Asian cookery, and although some varieties contain egg and are not suitable for vegans, most are perfect for vegetarian dishes. Mirin has a distinctive sweet-sour flavour and is easy to find in supermarkets and specialist food shops but you can achieve good results with a splash of sweet sherry, or cider vinegar that has been sweetened with a little sugar.

Five ways with asparagus

46

Steamed

Put the stalks into a standard steamer over a pan of boiling water, cover and steam for five minutes (or slightly longer if the stems are very thick). A simple dressing of melted butter or lemon oil is perfect – or go classical with hollandaise sauce (see page 85.)

47

As a salad

Cook the spears for two minutes in boiling water, drain and toss with vegetarian Parmesan-style cheese, lemon zest and olive oil. Add a poached egg or some crisp toast to create a complete lunch.

48

Over hot coals

Lay the spears out in a line, aligning the tips and trimming the bases. Push two or three skewers through the row at right angles to secure them, baste with oil and cook each side over hot coals.

49

On the griddle

Brush the spears with a little oil and lay them at right angles to the stripes in a griddle pan. Try not to move them about too much while they are cooking, so that you'll get the distinctive blackened stripes along the stem, along with a slightly smoky flavour.

50

As a stir-fry

Stir-fry the stems in a little oil for three minutes, then add 3 tablespoons of boiling water. Cover the pan and cook for a further three minutes, until the stems are tender. Serve on rice with crispy fried shallots.

51 Mushroom pilaf

Serves 4

Ingredients
- 1 onion
- 1 red pepper
- 115 g mixed mushrooms
- Few sprigs fresh parsley
- 280 g brown rice
- 2 tablespoons olive oil
- 600 ml vegetable stock
- 2 tablespoons flaked almonds

Preparation

Peel and chop the onion. De-seed and chop the red pepper. Wipe and slice the mixed mushrooms. Chop the parsley.

Warm the oil in a large saucepan and fry the onion and red pepper gently for five minutes, until soft and browning. Stir in the rice, mushrooms and stock. Bring to the boil, cover and simmer for 30 minutes, until the rice is tender and the liquid has been absorbed.

Just before serving, stir in the almonds and parsley.

You can use whichever mushrooms you prefer for this dish – button, chestnut and oyster mushrooms will all work well.

52 Spanish vegetable casserole

Serves 4

Ingredients
- 1 large onion
- 500 g new potatoes
- 3 cloves garlic
- 175 g fine green beans
- 1 firm pear
- 1 x 400 g tin chickpeas
- 2 tablespoons olive oil
- 1 tablespoon paprika
- 1 x 400 g tin chopped tomatoes
- 300 ml vegetable stock

Preparation

Peel and slice the onion. Cut the potatoes into bite-sized pieces. Peel and crush the garlic. Trim the beans and chop into short lengths. Core and chop the pear roughly. Drain and rinse the chickpeas.

In a large pan, fry the onion in the oil for two minutes, then stir in the potatoes, paprika and garlic. Cook, stirring constantly, for five minutes, then add the beans, pear, tomatoes, chickpeas and stock. Bring to the boil, then simmer, covered, for 30 minutes, until the potatoes are tender.

53 Basic crêpes
Makes 6

Ingredients
- 115 g plain flour
- Pinch salt
- 1 medium egg
- 300 ml milk
- Rapeseed oil, for frying

Preparation
Sift the flour and salt into a large mixing bowl. Make a well in the centre. Beat the egg and milk together, then gradually add the wet ingredients to the dry, beating thoroughly to remove any lumps. Alternatively, use a food processor to make a fast, smooth batter.

Heat a little oil in an medium-sized, shallow frying pan. Spoon approximately 2 tablespoons of the batter into the pan and carefully tip the pan so that the batter spreads out evenly. Cook on a high heat for a minute or two, until the bottom of the crêpe is no longer sticky. Turn and cook the other side before sliding onto a warmed plate. Repeat until all of the batter has been used.

Serve with lemon and sugar, or mix it up with one of the ideas opposite.

54 Ratatouille crêpe filling
Fills 4

Ingredients
- 225 g onions
- 2 cloves garlic
- 25 g courgettes
- 2 red peppers
- 1 x 400 g tin chickpeas
- Few sprigs fresh parsley
- Few sprigs fresh basil
- 1 tablespoon olive oil
- 1 x 400 g tin chopped tomatoes
- 1 tablespoon sun-dried tomato paste
- Salt and freshly ground black pepper

Preparation
Peel and roughly chop the onions. Peel and chop the garlic. Trim and slice the courgettes. De-seed and chop the peppers. Rinse and drain the chickpeas. Chop the fresh herbs.

Heat the oil in a large saucepan and fry the onions gently for three minutes. Add the garlic and cook for a further minute. Stir in all the remaining ingredients, season, cover and simmer for 30 minutes.

55 Soufflé crêpe filling
Fills 4

Ingredients
- 55 g Cheddar cheese
- 55 g walnuts
- 4 medium eggs
- 25 g salted butter
- 25 g plain flour
- 150 ml milk
- Salt and freshly ground black pepper

Preparation
Preheat the oven to 200°C. Grate the cheese and finely chop the walnuts. Beat two of the eggs. Separate the other two eggs into yolks and whites. Add one of the egg yolks to the two beaten eggs and beat again to mix thoroughly (the remaining egg yolk can be used for another recipe). Whisk the two egg whites together with a pinch of salt until they form stiff peaks.

Melt the butter in a large saucepan. Stir in the flour and cook for a minute, then gradually stir in the milk, keeping the pan on a low heat and beating constantly to prevent lumps as the mixture thickens. Take the pan off the heat and allow the mixture to cool a little. Add the beaten eggs, half the cheese and the seasoning, and beat together well. Transfer the mixture to a large mixing bowl and stir in the walnuts. Finally, gently fold in the beaten egg whites.

Put about 2 tablespoons of the soufflé mixture in a line down the centre of each pancake. Carefully fold them up and arrange in a greased baking dish, folded side down. Sprinkle with the remaining cheese and bake for up to 20 minutes, until puffy and bubbling. Serve immediately.

56 Crispy chickpea crêpes
Makes 8

Ingredients
- 225 g gram (chickpea) flour
- 1 tablespoon garam masala
- 1 teaspoon salt
- Pinch bicarbonate of soda
- Few sprigs fresh coriander
- Rapeseed oil, for frying

Preparation
Mix the flour, garam masala, salt and bicarbonate of soda together in a large bowl. Gradually add 400 ml water, beating constantly to make a smooth batter. Chop the coriander and add to the mix.

Heat a little oil in a large heavy-bottomed frying pan. Spoon 2 or 3 tablespoons of batter into the pan and quickly spread thinly using an oiled spatula. Lightly fry on both sides until crisp at the edges. Serve hot, alongside a dish of curried vegetables or folded around the Curried Baby Potatoes on page 33.

57 Walnut and avocado risotto
Serves 4

Ingredients
- 1.5 litres vegetable stock
- 1 onion
- 25 g salted butter
- 300 g Arborio or other short-grain rice
- 125 ml dry white wine
- 55 g vegetarian Parmesan-style cheese
- 2 ripe avocados
- 115 g walnut pieces
- Few fresh chives
- Few sprigs fresh parsley

Preparation
Put the stock into a pan and keep it warm on the stove. Peel and finely chop the onion. Melt the butter in a large saucepan and gently fry the onion for five minutes, until soft but not yet beginning to colour. Stir the rice into the onions, mix thoroughly and cook for about five minutes, stirring constantly, until the rice begins to look translucent. Pour in the wine and continue to stir until it is absorbed. Then begin to add the stock, a little at a time, stirring constantly over a low heat as the stock is absorbed. The process should take about 25 minutes and by the time the last of the stock is absorbed, the mixture should be thick and the rice tender.

Finely grate the cheese. Peel and dice the avocados. Put the walnut pieces into a dry, heavy-bottomed saucepan and heat them gently, stirring frequently, until they begin to colour, then turn onto a plate to stop them from cooking further. Chop the chives and parsley.

When the rice is ready, gently stir in the cheese, toasted walnuts and avocado pieces and serve immediately, garnished with the fresh herbs.

It's important to use risotto rice (such as Arborio or Carnaroli) as these short-grain rices absorb more moisture during cooking and release starch to create the authentic sticky texture of an Italian risotto.

58 Indian-spiced spring greens with coconut

Serves 4

Ingredients

- 450 g spring greens
- 2 green chillies
- Handful fresh coriander
- 2.5 cm ginger root
- Juice ½ lemon
- 1 tablespoon vegetable oil
- 1 teaspoon cumin seeds
- ½ teaspoon black mustard seeds
- 100 g fresh peas
- ½ teaspoon ground coriander
- 2 tablespoons desiccated coconut

Preparation

Wash and shred the spring greens. De-seed the chillies and chop finely. Roughly chop the fresh coriander. Peel and finely chop the ginger. Cut the lemon in half, juice one half and set aside.

Warm the oil in a large saucepan or wok, and gently toast the cumin seeds, mustard seeds, chopped chilli and ginger for two minutes.

Add the greens and the peas and then 2 tablespoons of water. Cover the pan and cook on a medium heat for five minutes.

Toss the lemon juice, ground coriander, half of the fresh coriander and half of the coconut into the greens. Mix well and serve immediately, topped with the remaining fresh coriander and coconut.

59 Spicy coconut rice

Serves 4

Ingredients

- 1 onion
- 1 red pepper
- 1 red chilli
- 225 g broccoli
- 2 tablespoons rapeseed oil
- 350 g basmati rice
- 140 ml coconut milk
- 600 ml vegetable stock
- 1 teaspoon garam masala
- 1 lime
- 2 tablespoons flaked almonds

Preparation

Peel and roughly chop the onion. De-seed the red pepper and cut it into slices. De-seed and finely chop the chilli. Cut the broccoli into small florets. Zest and juice the lime.

Heat the oil in a large pan or wok and stir-fry the vegetables for five minutes, until the onion is soft and translucent.

Add the rice, coconut milk and stock, stir to combine and bring to the boil. Reduce the heat and simmer very gently, without stirring, for up to 12 minutes, until the rice is cooked. Stir in the garam masala, flaked almonds and lime juice and zest. Heat through and serve immediately.

60 Thai stir-fry

Serves 4

Ingredients

- 1 onion
- 3 cloves garlic
- 1 chilli
- 2.5 cm ginger root
- 1 red pepper
- 1 green pepper
- 6 spring onions
- 100 g carrots
- 100 g spring greens
- 2 tablespoons soy sauce
- 1 tablespoon tomato purée
- 55 g pineapple chunks
- 115 g cashew nuts
- 3 tablespoons rapeseed oil
- 100 g mangetout

You can make the first steps of this recipe ahead of time, and then quickly stir-fry once your guests have arrived.

Preparation

Peel and slice the onion. Peel and crush the garlic. De-seed and very finely chop the chilli. Peel and finely chop the ginger. De-seed the peppers and slice them into strips. Trim and chop the spring onions. Peel and chop the carrots into thin matchsticks or slices. Wash and shred the greens.

Mix the soy sauce, tomato paste and any juice from the pineapple together in a small bowl or cup. Toast the cashews in a dry, heavy-bottomed saucepan for a few minutes until aromatic and browning, then remove from the heat.

Heat the oil in a wok. Add the onion, garlic, chilli and ginger. Stir-fry for one minute, then add the carrots, peppers, spring onions and mangetout. Stir-fry for two minutes, then add the pineapple chunks and the spring greens. Stir-fry for a further two minutes and, finally, add the soy sauce and tomato paste mixture and the nuts. Cook for one more minute to warm through and serve immediately.

61 Leek quiche

Serves 4

Ingredients
- 225 g leeks
- 25 g salted butter
- 1 pack ready-rolled puff pastry
- 6 medium eggs
- 225 g cottage cheese
- Salt and freshly ground black pepper
- Milk, to brush

Preparation
Preheat the oven to 180°C.

Trim and thinly slice the leeks. Melt the butter in a pan and gently fry the leeks until they are soft, about seven minutes.

Line a 23-cm quiche or pie dish with the pastry. Use the pastry trimmings to cut leaf shapes to decorate the edge of the quiche later.

Beat the eggs and cottage cheese together and season with salt and pepper. Stir in the cooked leeks, mix well and pour into the prepared quiche base. Decorate with the pastry leaves and brush with a little milk. Bake for up to 30 minutes, until the quiche is cooked through and the pie crust is golden.

Leeks are a traditional filling for the traditional French quiche, but here they are mixed with cottage cheese, which is lower in fat than hard cheeses like Cheddar.

62 Macaroni cheese with fennel

Serves 4

Ingredients

- 1 head fennel
- 55 g Cheddar cheese
- Few fresh chives
- 1 onion
- 300 ml milk
- 1 bay leaf
- 175 g wholewheat macaroni
- 40 g salted butter
- 25 g plain flour
- Freshly ground black pepper

This is my take on a traditional mac and cheese, which uses less cheese – so it is healthier, but just as tasty and comforting!

Preparation

Preheat the oven to 190°C.

Roughly chop the fennel, reserving any fronds for a garnish. Grate the cheese. Chop the fresh chives.

Peel the onion and cut it in half. Put it into a small saucepan with the milk and bay leaf. Bring to the boil, then remove from the heat and allow to stand for 15 minutes. Then remove and discard the onion and bay leaf.

Bring a large saucepan of salted water to the boil and cook the macaroni until just tender. Drain and set aside.

Melt the butter in a heavy-bottomed saucepan. Stir in the flour and cook for a minute before gradually adding the milk. Keep beating the mixture to prevent any lumps from forming. Bring the sauce to the boil, stirring continuously as it thickens. When the sauce has thickened, reduce the heat to a bare simmer, add half of the grated cheese and stir well to mix. When the cheese has melted into the sauce, stir in the macaroni, fennel and black pepper.

Transfer the mixture to a baking dish, top with the remaining cheese and bake for 25 minutes, until golden and bubbling. Sprinkle with fresh chopped chives and garnish with fennel fronds just before serving.

63 Mushroom and tomato spaghetti bake

Serves 4

Ingredients

- 115 g button mushrooms
- 1 onion
- 1 clove garlic
- Few sprigs fresh oregano
- 250 g wholewheat spaghetti
- 2 teaspoons olive oil
- 1 x 400 g tin chopped tomatoes
- 1 tablespoon sun-dried tomato paste
- 55 g Cheddar cheese

Preparation

Preheat the oven to 180°C.

Wipe and slice the mushrooms. Peel and roughly chop the onion and garlic. Chop the fresh oregano.

Bring a large saucepan of salted water to the boil and cook the spaghetti until tender. Drain and set aside.

Heat the oil in a pan and gently fry the onion for three minutes. Add the garlic and cook for a further minute or two. Stir in the mushrooms and cook, covered, for five more minutes. Add the tinned tomatoes, tomato paste and oregano and simmer gently for 10 minutes.

Mix the sauce into the spaghetti thoroughly and transfer to a baking dish. Grate the Cheddar cheese and sprinkle over the spaghetti. Bake for 25 minutes, until golden and bubbling.

Wholewheat spaghetti is a must for this dish, as it has a distinctive texture and will not turn to mush during cooking.

64 Asparagus tagliatelle

Serves 4

Ingredients

- 450 g asparagus
- 400 g fresh tagliatelle
- Small handful fresh, flat-leaf parsley
- Few sprigs fresh dill
- Few sprigs fresh chives
- 3 tablespoons lemon oil
- 1 tablespoon sea salt flakes

Preparation

Cut the asparagus into short pieces – using just the tips is prettiest for this dish, but you can use the stems too, or reserve them for another dish. Prepare a large saucepan of boiling salted water, with a steamer on top. Cook the pasta in the water, and at the same time, steam the asparagus tips. Both the pasta and the asparagus tips should be ready in around five minutes. While cooking, chop the herbs.

Drain the pasta and arrange it on four serving plates, topped with the asparagus, chopped herbs, lemon oil and a sprinkle of sea salt flakes, to taste.

Tagliatelle are long flat ribbons of pasta, sometimes coloured with spinach or tomato. They are often sold dried in small 'nests' – take care to loosen them when cooking in boiling water, so that they cook evenly.

65 Spaghetti with lemon and parsley

Serves 4

Ingredients
- 85 g vegetarian Parmesan-style cheese
- Small handful fresh parsley
- 300 g dried spaghetti
- 25 g salted butter
- Zest 1 lemon
- Freshly ground black pepper

Preparation
Grate the cheese finely and chop the parsley.
Bring a large saucepan of salted water to the boil
and cook the spaghetti until tender. Drain and toss
with the butter, cheese, parsley, lemon zest and
black pepper. Serve immediately.

*This simple dish will become a family favourite –
fresh lemon zest and parsley bring the flavours to life.
Traditional Parmesan and Grana Padano cheeses are
made with animal rennet so look for a hard cheese
that is labelled 'suitable for vegetarians'.*

66 Spring vegetables with tarragon mayonnaise

Serves 4

Ingredients

- 115 g broccoli
- 115 g baby carrots
- 115 g sugar snap peas
- 115 g mangetout
- 115 g courgettes
- 115 g fresh peas

For the mayonnaise

- 4 medium eggs
- Small handful fresh tarragon
- 2 teaspoons mild mustard
- 1 tablespoon white wine vinegar
- 600 ml vegetable oil
- Salt and freshly ground white pepper

Preparation

Cut the broccoli into small florets and halve any thick carrots. Steam the broccoli, carrots, sugar snap peas and mangetout for 10 minutes, until just tender. Thinly slice the courgettes.

Make the mayonnaise. Separate the egg yolks from the whites (you can save the whites for another dish). Finely chop the tarragon.

Put the egg yolks into a blender with the mustard and vinegar. Switch the machine on and gradually pour in the oil. The mixture should emulsify and thicken as you watch. Spoon the mayonnaise out of the blender and transfer to a small mixing bowl. Stir in the chopped tarragon and season to taste with salt and pepper.

Serve the steamed vegetables, along with the raw peas and courgette slices, arranged on a plate with a little pot of mayonnaise, or mix all the vegetables together in a large bowl and toss the mayonnaise through immediately before serving.

Five ways with artichokes

67

Steamed

Cut off the stalks and boil standing up in a large saucepan with a splash of salt and lemon. Cover and cook for 40 minutes or until a leaf can easily be pulled off. Turn out upside down to drain and set aside. They are best served tepid. Mix mustard and wine vinegar with olive oil, season with salt and sugar, and serve as a dip.

68

Fried

Prepare and cook artichokes as above, then fry the hearts (one per person) with mushrooms. Dress with sherry vinegar. Serve with baby romaine salad and cherry tomatoes.

69

Grilled

Prepare and cook artichokes as above, then cut them in half lengthways; remove the choke, brush with oil and grill until lightly charred. Serve with the dressing from recipe 67, with added honey.

70

Roasted

Prepare as above, cut into halves and remove the choke. Drizzle with oil and a squeeze of lemon and roast in the oven at 200°C for about 40 minutes, or until golden brown.

71

Stuffed

Prepare the artichoke as above, then fill the centre with a mixture of breadcrumbs, vegetarian Parmesan-style cheese, garlic and herbs of your choice, and steam.

72 Oriental omelette parcels

Serves 4

Ingredients
- 3 medium eggs
- 1 tablespoon mirin (Japanese rice wine)
- 1 teaspoon toasted sesame oil
- Vegetable oil, for frying
- Salt and freshly ground black pepper

For the filling
- Large handful beansprouts
- 3 spring onions
- 1 carrot
- 2 radishes
- 1 tablespoon toasted sesame oil
- 1 tablespoon soy sauce

Preparation
Break the eggs into a bowl and beat together well with the mirin and sesame oil. Season to taste with salt and black pepper. Heat a little oil in a frying pan and use the mixture to make four thin omelettes. Interleave the omelettes with baking parchment and keep in the oven on a very low heat while you prepare the filling.

Trim and finely slice the spring onions. Grate the carrot and radishes. Warm the sesame oil in a wok and stir-fry the vegetables for one minute, until heated through but still crisp. Splash the soy sauce into the warm mixture and toss through.

Divide the warm stir-fried mixture between the omelettes and fold like parcels to serve.

Japanese rice wine (mirin) adds a sweetness to these omelettes, while toasted sesame oil has a distinctive nutty flavour that works well with all kinds of stir-fried vegetable dishes.

73 Leek risotto torte

Serves 4

Ingredients

- 450 g leeks
- 1 onion
- 3 cloves garlic
- Small handful fresh basil
- 55 g salted butter
- 225 g Arborio or other short-grain rice
- 200 ml dry white wine
- 450 ml warm vegetable stock
- 2 medium eggs
- 55 ml crème fraîche
- 100 g vegetarian Parmesan-style cheese
- Salt and freshly ground black pepper

Preparation

Trim and finely slice the leeks. Peel and chop the onion. Peel and chop the garlic. Chop the fresh basil. Melt the butter in a large saucepan and gently fry the leeks, onion and garlic for two minutes. Stir in the rice and cook for a further two minutes until the rice starts to become translucent. Add the wine and cook, stirring constantly, until it has been absorbed by the rice.

Add the stock a little at a time, stirring constantly, allowing it to be absorbed by the rice. Adding all the stock will take about 25 minutes and then the rice will be cooked and thickened.

Preheat the oven to 200°C and grease and line a 20-cm round cake tin.

Beat the eggs and mix them into the risotto with the fresh basil, crème fraîche, cheese and seasoning. Spoon into the pan, smooth the top and bake for up to 25 minutes, until firm and golden. Leave to cool slightly before turning out of the tin and slicing.

74 Turkish turlu turlu

Serves 4

Ingredients

- 1 aubergine
- 100 g okra
- 300 g green beans
- 2 onions
- 1 green pepper
- 4 courgettes
- 400 g potatoes
- 4 to 5 fresh tomatoes
- Large handful fresh parsley
- 250 g peas
- 1 x 400 g tin tomatoes
- 6 tablespoons olive oil
- Salt and freshly ground black pepper
- 2 teaspoons paprika

Preparation

Preheat the oven to 190°C.

Cut the aubergine into cubes, place in a colander and sprinkle with salt. Leave for 30 minutes, then rinse and pat dry with kitchen towel.

Trim the okra, removing the stalks, and trim the beans. Peel and roughly chop the onions. De-seed and roughly chop the pepper. Trim and slice the courgette. Peel the potatoes and chop into bite-sized chunks. Slice the fresh tomatoes. Chop the parsley.

Put the prepared aubergine, okra, peas, beans, courgettes, onions, potatoes, peppers, parsley and tinned tomatoes in a casserole dish. Pour over 4 tablespoons of olive oil, season with salt, pepper and paprika and mix together thoroughly. Smooth out the top of the mixture and cover with slices of tomato. Finish with the remaining olive oil.

Bake for 60 minutes, until the tomatoes are starting to brown. Serve with fresh bread.

75 Thai green curry

Serves 4

For the curry paste

- 1 stalk lemongrass
- 2 to 3 green chillies, to taste
- 5 cm ginger root
- 4 to 5 cloves garlic
- 1 shallot
- Large handful fresh coriander
- 3 kaffir lime leaves, optional
- 100 ml coconut milk
- 1 tablespoon soy sauce
- 2 tablespoons lime juice
- 1 tablespoon sugar
- ½ teaspoon ground cumin
- ½ teaspoon ground coriander
- Salt and freshly ground white pepper to taste

For the curry

- Vegetable oil, for stir-frying
- 1 x 400 g tin chickpeas
- 200 ml vegetable stock
- 1 green or red pepper
- 1 aubergine, or 4 Thai aubergines
- 300 ml coconut milk
- 200 g firm tofu
- 115 g sliced bamboo shoots

Preparation

Make the curry paste first. Trim and finely slice the lemongrass. De-seed and chop the chillies, peel and slice the ginger, garlic and the shallot, and chop the coriander. Put all the curry paste ingredients into a food processor and blend to a smooth paste.

Chop the vegetables into bite-sized pieces. Warm the vegetable oil in a wok and add the curry paste. Heat it through, stirring constantly, for one minute, then add the drained, rinsed chickpeas, vegetable stock and aubergine and simmer for five minutes. Drain and pat dry the tofu and cut into strips. Stir in the pepper, tofu and bamboo shoots and cook gently for a few minutes. When the vegetables are softened but still quite firm, stir in the tomatoes and coconut milk, and heat through. Serve immediately, garnished with fresh herbs.

76 Beans bourguignon

Serves 4

Ingredients

- 1 onion
- 2 cloves garlic
- 1 large carrot
- 1 large potato
- 225 g mushrooms
- 2 tablespoons olive oil
- 3 tablespoons tomato purée
- 1 teaspoon dried thyme
- 2 bay leaves
- 1 x 400 g tin haricot beans
- 300 ml red wine
- 25 g salted butter
- Salt and freshly ground black pepper

Preparation

Peel and chop the onion. Peel and crush the garlic. Peel the carrot and potato. Chop the carrot into thin slices and the potato into small cubes. Wipe and slice the mushrooms.

Warm the olive oil in a flameproof casserole dish and fry the onion for three minutes. Stir in the potato and carrot. Add 225 ml of water. Stir in the tomato paste, thyme and bay leaves. Bring to the boil and cook for 15 minutes. Add the beans, wine and garlic. Turn the heat down and simmer gently for a further 10 minutes. Remove the bay leaves.

Melt the butter in a frying pan and gently fry the mushrooms for up to three minutes. Stir them into the beans and adjust the seasoning with salt and pepper before serving.

A tasty classic French sauce made with herbs and red wine makes an inexpensive dish of beans into a more sophisticated offering!

77 Vegetable casserole with apricots

Serves 4

Ingredients

- 1 onion
- 2 cloves garlic
- 1 head celery
- 3 courgettes
- 1 yellow pepper
- 1 green pepper
- 12 dried apricots
- 3 tablespoons olive oil
- 1 teaspoon turmeric
- 1 bay leaf
- 1 x 400 g tin chopped tomatoes
- 1 x 400 g tin chickpeas
- 300 ml vegetable stock
- Pinch cayenne pepper
- Salt and freshly ground black pepper

Preparation

Peel and roughly chop the onion. Peel and crush the garlic. Trim and roughly chop the celery, courgette and peppers. Chop the apricots into quarters.

Warm the oil in a large flameproof casserole dish and gently fry the onion, garlic, celery, peppers, turmeric and bay leaf for five minutes. Add the apricots, tomatoes, chickpeas and stock; cover and simmer for 30 minutes. Season to taste with cayenne, salt and pepper.

78 Mexican chickpeas with paprika

Serves 4

Ingredients

- 3 onions
- 4 cloves garlic
- 4 tablespoons olive oil
- 1 teaspoon cayenne pepper
- 2 teaspoons ground coriander
- 2 teaspoons ground cumin
- 2 teaspoons paprika
- 1 teaspoon turmeric
- 1 pound dried chickpeas
- 450 ml vegetable stock
- 1 x 400 g tin chopped tomatoes
- 2 tablespoons tomato paste

Preparation

Peel and roughly chop the onions. Peel and crush the garlic. Gently fry the onion and garlic in the oil for five minutes in a large saucepan until the onion is soft. Stir in the cayenne, coriander, cumin, paprika and turmeric and cook for a further minute before adding the chickpeas, stock, tomatoes and tomato paste. Bring to the boil, then reduce the heat, cover and simmer for one hour, until the chickpeas are cooked. This dish can be served hot or cold.

If using tinned chickpeas, cook for 15 minutes rather than the full hour.

79 Spicy bean casserole

Serves 4

Ingredients

- 1 onion
- 1 clove garlic
- 1 courgette
- 1 green pepper
- 1 x 400 g tin haricot beans
- 1 x 400 g tin kidney beans
- 2 tablespoons olive oil
- 25 g plain flour
- 1 teaspoon mild chilli powder
- 1 x 400 g tin chopped tomatoes
- 1 teaspoon sun-dried tomato paste
- 150 ml vegetable stock
- 100 g sweetcorn
- Salt and freshly ground black pepper

Preparation

Peel and roughly chop the onion. Peel and crush the garlic. Trim and slice the courgette. De-seed and slice the pepper. Drain and rinse the tinned beans.

Gently fry the onion and garlic in the oil for five minutes, until soft. Stir in the flour, chilli powder, tinned tomatoes and tomato paste, then gradually add the stock, stirring to prevent any lumps from forming. Add the courgette, peppers, beans and sweetcorn and bring to the boil. Reduce the heat and simmer, covered, for 10 minutes, until the courgette is tender.

Season to taste and serve hot.

80 Easy-baked brown rice

Serves 4

Ingredients

- 2 onions
- 3 cloves garlic
- 2.5 cm ginger root
- 4 cardamom pods
- 1 cinnamon stick
- 2 tablespoons rapessed oil
- 1 teaspoon cumin seeds
- 1 teaspoon coriander seeds
- 250 g brown long-grain rice
- 450 ml vegetable stock
- Handful fresh, chopped coriander

Preparation

Preheat oven to 150°C .

Peel and thinly slice the onions. Peel and slice the garlic. Grate the ginger. Lightly crush the cardamom pods and cinnamon stick.

Put the onion, garlic, ginger and oil into a flameproof casserole dish and fry gently for two minutes. Add all the remaining ingredients except the coriander. Stir to mix, then cover with a lid or kitchen foil and bake in the oven for one hour. Garnish with the coriander to serve.

Five ways with peas

81

Straight from the garden

There is no need to cook freshly picked peas. Enjoy them raw as part of a fresh salad. Their sweetness contrasts well with the earthy taste of baby beetroots and the lemony tang of feta cheese.

82

Pea shoots

A pretty and versatile addition to salads, pea shoots are easy to grow, even if you don't have a garden. Simply plant whole dried peas in shallow trays, water regularly and watch them shoot up. Harvest when they are about 7.5 cm tall, before they start to tangle together.

83

Pea purée

Purée fresh peas with fresh mint and a little melted butter, and serve as a side dish. Or you can blend lemon juice, black pepper, breadcrumbs and vegetarian ricotta cheese for a smooth pâté.

84

Cocktail fritters

Stir into a thick, well-seasoned batter and deep-fry to make bite-sized cocktail snacks, perfect for the year's first outdoor gatherings.

85

Pea shooters

Make a light pea and mint soup, chill and add a splash of lemon vodka. Serve as a starter in chilled shot glasses garnished with fresh pea shoots.

86 Spring fling
Serves 4

Ingredients
- ½ cucumber
- 3 lemons
- Handful fresh mint
- 3 to 4 tablespoons white sugar, to taste
- 250 ml vodka
- 4 teaspoons caster sugar
- 250 ml sparkling mineral water

Preparation
Thinly slice the cucumber and one of the lemons. Juice the remaining lemons. Chop the mint roughly.

Put the cucumber and lemon slices, lemon juice, vodka, mint and sugar in a large jug. Cover and chill for 30 minutes.

Stir the mixture to help dissolve the sugar and chill for a further 30 minutes. Add the water and serve over ice in long glasses.

87 Fruit cooler
Serves 4

Ingredients
- 400 ml pineapple juice
- 400 ml orange juice
- 400 ml grapefruit juice
- 125 ml grenadine syrup

Preparation
Mix all the ingredients together in a big jug with lots of ice!

88 Rhubarb and ginger cordial

Serves 4

Ingredients
- 280 g rhubarb
- 5 cm ginger root
- Juice 1 lemon
- 1 orange
- 250 g caster sugar

Preparation

Trim the rhubarb and cut it into 2.5-cm pieces. Peel and roughly chop the ginger. Zest and juice the orange.

Put the sugar, rhubarb, lemon juice, orange zest and juice, and ginger into a large pan with 300 ml of water. Warm the pan to dissolve the sugar, then bring to the boil. Boil for five minutes, then remove from the heat and leave to cool. Strain through a muslin cloth and store in a sterilised bottle in the refrigerator. Serve mixed with sparkling mineral water.

89 Spring tonic smoothie

Serves 4

Ingredients
- 1 large ripe banana
- 85 g spinach
- 85 g blueberries
- 85 g strawberries
- 475 ml cold milk
  or non-dairy alternative

Preparation

Peel and chop the banana. Shred the spinach. Blend all the ingredients together in a blender or food processor.

90 Rhubarb and mascarpone filo purses

Serves 4

Ingredients
- 2 tablespoons stem ginger in syrup
- 225 g mascarpone cheese
- 2 tablespoons desiccated coconut
- 1 stick forced pink rhubarb
- 40 g salted butter
- 3 sheets filo pastry
- 2 tablespoons sugar

For the coulis
- 1 stick forced pink rhubarb
- 100 g ripe strawberries
- 100 g caster sugar

Preparation
Preheat the oven to 200°C.

Chop the ginger finely and mix it into the mascarpone. Add the coconut and mix well. Trim the rhubarb and slice into pieces no more than 1-cm thick.

Melt the butter and brush half of it over one sheet of pastry. Cover with a second sheet of pastry, brush with butter and top with the third pastry sheet. Use a sharp knife to cut the pastry into four equal squares, working quickly so that the pastry doesn't dry out. Divide the mascarpone mixture between the pastry pieces, press in some of the rhubarb and finish with sugar. Bring the corners of the pastry up and squeeze together to seal into a purse shape. Transfer to a baking tray lined with baking parchment and bake for 10 minutes, until the pastry is golden.

To make the coulis, trim and finely chop the rhubarb. Finely chop the strawberries. Place the fruit into a small saucepan with the sugar and cook gently for 10 minutes, until the sugar has dissolved and the fruit is meltingly soft. Pass the mixture through a sieve. Spoon a pool of the coulis onto a serving plate and place the filo purse on top. Serve immediately.

91 Classic lemon tart

Serves 8

Ingredients

- 85 g unsalted butter
- 175 g plain flour
- 1 tablespoon icing sugar
- 1 medium egg yolk

For the filling

- Juice 3 lemons
- 25 g cornflour
- 3 medium egg yolks
- 115 g caster sugar
- 150 ml double cream
- Zest 1 lemon

Preparation

Cut the butter into small pieces and rub it into the flour with your fingertips. Stir in the icing sugar and the egg yolk and mix well. Gradually add cold water, a splash at a time, until the dough comes together and is soft but not sticky. Gather into a ball, wrap in a plastic food bag and chill for 20 minutes.

Preheat the oven to 190°C. Roll the pastry out thinly and line a 20- to 23-cm fluted pie tin. Prick the base and leave to rest for a further 20 minutes. Then line the base with baking parchment and fill with baking beans.

Bake for 15 minutes, then remove the beans and paper and return to the oven for five more minutes. Set aside. Turn the oven temperature down to 180°C.

To make the filling, add enough cold water to the lemon juice to make 450 ml. Transfer to a small pan and beat in the cornflour. Turn on the heat and gradually bring the mixture to the boil, stirring constantly. When the consistency is like a thick sauce, take the pan off the heat and allow the mixture to cool. Beat in the egg yolks, sugar, cream and lemon zest, and return the pan to the heat. Gradually bring to the boil, stirring constantly. As soon as it begins to bubble, pour it into the pastry crust and bake for 20 minutes. Cool and chill thoroughly before slicing.

92 Lattice-topped custard tart
Serves 6

Ingredients
- 125 g cold unsalted butter
- 175 g plain flour
- 50 g caster sugar
- 1 medium egg yolk
- 2 tablespoons raspberry jam

For the filling
- 2 medium eggs plus 1 egg yolk
- 350 ml milk
- 2 tablespoons soft brown sugar
- ½ teaspoon ground nutmeg
- 1 tablespoon pine nuts
- Milk for glazing
- Icing sugar, to serve

Preparation
Preheat the oven to 200°C. Cut the butter into small pieces and rub it into the flour using your fingertips. Stir in the sugar and then mix in the egg yolk. If the dough doesn't come together, add a splash of water. Turn onto a floured surface and knead for about three minutes, until smooth. Wrap in a plastic food bag and chill for 30 minutes.

Roll the pastry out thinly and line a deep, 20-cm pie dish. Save the trimmings for later. Refrigerate the pastry shell for a further 10 minutes, then line it with baking parchment and fill it with baking beans. Bake for 10 minutes, then remove the beans and parchment and bake for a further six minutes or so until it begins to colour. Set aside and turn the oven down to 180°C. When the pastry shell has cooled a little, brush the base with raspberry preserve.

To make the custard, whisk the eggs, egg yolk, milk, sugar and nutmeg together. Pour into the pastry shell and bake for 25 minutes. Re-roll the pastry trimmings, then cut into long strips approximately 2.5 cm wide. Remove the tart from the oven and arrange the strips in a lattice over the top. Sprinkle with pine nuts, brush with a little milk and return to the oven for a further 20 minutes, until just set. Dust with icing sugar before serving.

Summer

Fresh in Season ...

Tomatoes

The quintessential summer food – they are never as good at any other time of year, and are best still warm from the sun. Look out for yellow and orange tomatoes and interesting heritage varieties. Simply slice, top with quality olive oil and basil, and serve with good bread.

Courgettes

Courgettes should be dark green and glossy, with no soft spots. Baby courgettes are a seasonal delicacy – quarter them lengthways and serve raw with an aioli dip. Larger specimens are great halved and grilled on the barbecue.

New potatoes

Baby new potatoes are a summer treat, making a salad into a satisfying meal. Choose small, regular-sized potatoes with flaking, papery skins and scrub them (no need to peel). Top with good salted butter or a dollop of vegan mayonnaise.

Aubergines

Aubergines should be firm and smooth, with a uniform dark colour. They're a barbecue favourite – grill until the skins are black, scoop out the soft flesh and mash with tahini and minced garlic to make a dip that's great hot or cold.

Radishes

Too often confined to the salad bowl, radishes add delicious fresh peppery flavour to sandwiches, picnics and stir-fries. For a stylish starter, serve small radishes whole, with olive oil and sea salt to dip into.

Avocados

Choose avocados that are neither rock hard nor too soft. If they ripen more before you are ready to eat them, mash them into a guacamole. Firm avocados can be halved, de-stoned, filled with a savoury nut mixture and baked.

Cucumbers

Cucumbers should be dark green and very firm. Keep them in the refrigerator and if they are wrapped in plastic, leave it on to maximise shelf life. Cold slices of cucumber are great for quickly cooling tall summer drinks.

Peppers

Like cucumbers, tomatoes and courgettes, these summer veggies are strictly fruits! Try adding crisp, chilled slices to colourful summer salads or stuff them, wrap them in foil and bake or barbecue until soft and juicy.

93 Mango and sunflower seed pâté

Serves 4

Ingredients
- 140 g sunflower seeds
- 1 ripe mango
- ½ jalapeño pepper
- 1 clove garlic
- 1 tablespoon soy sauce
- Juice of ½ lime
- 1 spring onion

Preparation
Cover the sunflower seeds with water and soak for eight hours or overnight. Drain and rinse them.

Peel, stone and finely chop the mango. De-seed and finely chop the jalapeño pepper. Peel and crush the garlic. Finely chop the spring onion. Put the seeds into a food processor with the jalapeño, garlic, soy sauce and lime juice and blend until smooth. Transfer to a bowl and mix in the mango and chopped spring onion. Serve chilled with crackers or crusty bread.

94 New season baby potato salad

Serves 4

Ingredients
- 1 clove garlic
- 175 g small Jersey Royal new potatoes
- 55 g salted butter
- 100 g fresh watercress
- 2 teaspoons balsamic vinegar

Preparation
Peel and crush the garlic. Boil the potatoes in salted water until tender. Drain and thickly slice. Return to the warm pan along with the butter and garlic, and toss together to melt the butter. Cool to room temperature and then refrigerate for at least an hour so that the butter sets. Trim the watercress and chop it into short lengths. To serve, toss the potatoes with the watercress and balsamic vinegar.

To make this feature salad, you should look out for the first crop of new potatoes to arrive in the shops.

95 Spanish watermelon soup

Serves 4

Ingredients

- 800 g ripe, seedless watermelon
- 4 tomatoes
- 1 clove garlic
- 3 slices white bread
- 55 g toasted flaked almonds
- 2 tablespoons olive oil
- 2 tablespoons red wine vinegar
- ½ teaspoon paprika
- ½ teaspoon ground cumin
- Salt and freshly ground black pepper

Preparation

Roughly chop the watermelon. Peel and chop the tomatoes. Peel and crush the garlic. Put the bread onto a plate and cover with water – allow to soak for five minutes, then squeeze the bread to remove excess moisture.

Put the bread into the bowl of a food processor with the tomatoes, almonds, olive oil, vinegar, garlic, paprika and cumin. Process until smooth, then add the watermelon and process again. Strain the mixture through a fine sieve, season to taste and chill thoroughly before serving.

This refreshing chilled soup is thickened with bread and almonds, which makes it a light but satisfying summertime meal.

96 Chunky gazpacho

Serves 4

Ingredients

- 3 large ripe tomatoes
- 2 ripe avocados
- 1 small red onion
- 1 green chilli
- 1 clove garlic
- Handful fresh coriander
- Handful fresh parsley
- Handful fresh basil
- Juice 1 lime
- Salt and freshly ground black pepper
- Ice cubes, to serve

Preparation

Roughly chop the tomatoes. Peel, stone and chop the avocados. Peel and chop the onion. Peel and chop the garlic. De-seed and finely chop the chilli. Chop the herbs. Put all of the ingredients into the bowl of a food processor and pulse to combine. You are aiming for a chunky consistency, not a purée. Season to taste with salt and pepper. Chill for an hour and top each serving with a cube or two of ice.

Five ways with cucumber

97
Sandwiches
Cut the cucumber lengthways, scoop out the seeds and finely slice. Sprinkle with salt and leave in a colander for 30 minutes. Rinse under ice-cold water, pat dry and sandwich between thinly sliced, buttered white bread, with the crusts cut off.

98
Soups
Slice and fry cucumber with some garlic and onions, then purée. Loosen with vegetable stock, white wine and cream, then flavour to taste with fresh herbs – mint is a favourite.

99
Cocktails
Flavour gin or vodka by putting peeled, de-seeded and chopped cucumber into a large jar, covering with the alcohol, sealing and leaving to steep for a week. Strain, and use to make cocktails.

100
Raita
Cucumber raita is a cooling Indian dip made from grated cucumber and plain yogurt, often with finely chopped mint or fresh green chilli. Serve with chillies, tagines, Mexican dishes and spicy barbecues.

101
Stir-fries
Cucumber is rarely served cooked, but this works well in Asian menus. Slice into very fine ribbons and stir-fry for two minutes with a little soy sauce, garlic and toasted sesame oil. Serve as a side dish or in place of noodles.

102 Asparagus spears with hollandaise sauce

Serves 4

Ingredients

- 1 bunch asparagus
- 1 tablespoon vegetable oil
- 2 tablespoons lemon juice
- 175 ml skimmed milk
- 1 tablespoon salted butter
- 1 teaspoon cornflour
- Salt and freshly ground black pepper
- 1 medium egg

Preparation

Bend the asparagus stems until they snap naturally. Discard the lower woody ends. Bring a large saucepan of salted water to the boil. Plunge the asparagus into the water, cook for around three minutes, then drain. Serve immediately or toss with a little vegetable oil and cook in a hot griddle pan, until the asparagus spears are marked with deep brown lines.

To make the hollandaise sauce, mix half the lemon juice with the milk. Melt the butter in a small pan, cook for a minute until it is golden, then pour into a small bowl and set aside.

Put 4 tablespoons of the milk and lemon mixture into a small bowl or cup and mix in the cornflour, salt and pepper, stirring well to prevent any lumps from forming. Warm the remaining milk in a heavy-bottomed saucepan, and gradually add the cornflour mixture and the egg, beating continuously. Continue to cook the sauce over a medium heat until it reaches simmering point. Remove from the heat and beat in the remaining lemon juice and the melted butter. Serve immediately with the asparagus.

103 Broad bean and mozzarella bruschetta

Serves 4

Ingredients
- 250 g podded broad beans
- 3 tablespoons olive oil
- Juice 1 lemon
- Handful fresh mint
- Salt and freshly ground black pepper
- 4 slices crusty bread
- 1 clove garlic
- 140 g mozzarella cheese

Preparation

Bring a pan of salted water to the boil. Plunge the beans into the boiling water, cook for two minutes and, using a slotted spoon, scoop them out of the hot water and into a bowl of cold water. Peel away and discard the skins. Roughly crush the beans with the olive oil and lemon juice. Chop the mint and mix into the paste. Season with salt and pepper.

Toast the bread. Peel the garlic, then rub the crisp surface of the toasted bread with the whole garlic clove. Top each slice of bread with the bean mixture, tear the mozzarella into small pieces and scatter over the bruschetta.

Broad beans look so much more alluring when you take the time to pop them out of their skins! They make a purée that is smoother and more colourful, too.

104 Minted lettuce soup

Serves 4

Ingredients
- 4 shallots
- 1 clove garlic
- 200 g new potatoes
- 1 Little Gem lettuce
- Small handful fresh mint
- 55 g salted butter
- 900 ml vegetable stock
- 115 g fresh or frozen peas
- Salt and freshly ground black pepper
- 150 ml single cream

Preparation

Peel and finely chop the shallots. Peel and crush the garlic. Finely slice the potatoes. Shred the lettuce and chop the mint.

Melt the butter in a large saucepan and gently cook the shallots until soft and translucent. Add the garlic and cook for another minute, then stir in the potatoes and stock. Bring to the boil, reduce the heat and simmer, covered, until the potatoes are falling apart, around 15 minutes. Add the lettuce, mint and peas and cook for five more minutes; leave to cool.

Transfer to a food processor and blend until smooth. Season to taste with salt and pepper, and chill. Swirl the single cream into the cold soup just before serving.

105 Summer day salad

Serves 4

Ingredients
- 1 mango
- 1 avocado
- 2 carrots
- 6 spring onions
- 1 clove garlic
- 2.5 cm ginger root
- 2 tablespoons rapeseed oil
- 2 tablespoons lime juice
- Seeds of ½ pomegranate
- Salt and freshly ground black pepper

Preparation

Peel, stone and slice the mango and the avocado. Peel the carrots, if necessary, and slice as thinly as possible. Trim and slice the spring onions. Peel and crush the garlic. Peel and grate the ginger. Combine the oil and lime juice and mix in the grated ginger and garlic. Put all the ingredients into a large serving bowl and toss well to combine. Season and serve immediately.

Pomegranate seeds are so beautiful, they add a splash of colour to all sorts of dishes. Simply cut the fruit in half and delve with your fingers to free them from the white pith.

106 Mushroom, rocket and red kidney bean salad

Serves 4

Ingredients
- 1 x 200 g tin kidney beans
- 1 red onion
- 115 g button mushrooms
- 70 g rocket

For the dressing
- 1 tablespoon soy sauce
- 2 tablespoons olive oil
- Juice 1 lemon
- 1 teaspoon honey
- Salt and freshly ground black pepper

Preparation
Rinse and drain the kidney beans. Peel the onion and slice it finely. Wipe and slice the mushrooms. Chop the rocket roughly. Make the dressing by mixing all the ingredients together.

Arrange the rocket on a serving dish. Mix the dressing with the mushrooms, onion and beans, and arrange them on top of the rocket to serve.

107 Melon and mozzarella skewers

Serves 4

Ingredients
- ½ cantaloupe melon
- 4 spring onions
- 2 packs (approx. 250 g) of mini mozzarella balls

Preparation
De-seed the melon, and use a melon baller to cut as many melon balls as you can. Trim the spring onions and cut them into short lengths. Drain the mozzarella balls. Using toothpicks, assemble mini skewers with melon balls, mozzarella balls and pieces of spring onion.

108 Caponata Siciliana
Serves 4

Ingredients
- 450 g aubergine
- 1 onion
- 1 celery heart
- 15 g capers
- 4 tablespoons olive oil
- 1 x 200 g tin chopped tomatoes
- 25 g pine nuts
- 100 g pitted black olives
- Salt and freshly ground black pepper
- 2 teaspoons brown sugar
- 2 tablespoons red wine vinegar

Preparation
Trim and chop the aubergine into small cubes. Peel and chop the onion. Chop the celery finely, place in a colander and pour over a kettle of boiling water to blanch it. Rinse the capers in water.

Heat half of the oil in a large saucepan and fry the aubergine until brown, about five minutes. Remove the aubergine from the pan and set aside. Pour the remaining oil into the pan and gently fry the onion until soft. Stir in the blanched celery, chopped tomatoes, pine nuts, olives and capers and fry gently until the celery is cooked, about five minutes. Season with salt and pepper.

Mix the aubergine into the sauce, add the sugar and vinegar and cook gently for a further 10 minutes. Serve warm or cold with crackers or breadsticks.

109 Hot pepper salsa
Serves 4

Ingredients
- 1 yellow pepper
- 4 tomatoes
- 1 or 2 hot yellow or red chillies
- ½ onion
- 2 cloves garlic
- Juice 1 lime
- 2 tablespoons white wine vinegar
- ½ teaspoon salt

Preparation
De-seed and finely chop the pepper, tomatoes and chillies. Peel and finely chop the onion. Peel and crush the garlic. Put all the ingredients into a pan and cook gently for 15 minutes. Leave to cool before serving.

Yellow and orange tomatoes look wonderful in this dish, if they are available. The heat of the salsa depends on your choice of chillies!

110 Chilled tomato soup

Serves 4

Ingredients
- 900 g ripe tomatoes
- 1 onion
- 1 clove garlic
- 25 g salted butter
- 1 teaspoon brown sugar
- Pinch cayenne pepper
- Salt and freshly ground black pepper

Preparation
Roughly chop the tomatoes. Peel and chop the onion and the garlic. Melt the butter in a large saucepan and gently fry the onions until they are soft. Stir in the garlic and cook for a few minutes more, then add the tomatoes. Cook over a medium heat, stirring frequently, until the tomatoes are beginning to disintegrate.

Mix in 350 ml of water, the sugar and the cayenne pepper and simmer for 10 more minutes. Cool, then transfer to a food processor and blend until very smooth. Season to taste, then chill thoroughly before serving.

Tomato soup does not have to be hot, especially at this time of year. The most famous chilled soup is Spanish tomato gazpacho, but this one is a little different.

111 Spinach salad with beetroot and haricot beans

Serves 4

Ingredients
- 450 g baby leaf spinach
- 1 red onion
- 4 small pickled beetroots
- 1 x 400 g tin haricot beans

For the dressing
- 2 cloves garlic
- 5 tablespoons olive oil
- 2 tablespoons red wine vinegar
- 1 teaspoon Dijon mustard
- Salt and freshly ground black pepper

Preparation
Shred the spinach. Peel and very finely slice the onion. Slice the beetroots thinly. Drain and rinse the haricot beans.

To make the dressing, peel and crush the garlic and combine with all the remaining ingredients. Beat together.

Arrange the spinach on a serving dish, top with the beetroot and beans and pour the dressing over the top. Serve immediately.

112 Apple, pineapple and cheese salad

Serves 4

Ingredients
- 3 apples
- Juice 1 lemon
- ½ red onion
- 450 g fresh pineapple
- 200 g Cheddar cheese
- 4 tablespoons sour cream
- 2 tablespoons mayonnaise

Preparation
Core and slice the apples and place in a bowl with the lemon juice to prevent them from browning. Peel and finely chop the onion. Cut the pineapple into bite-sized pieces. Grate the cheese. Mix the sour cream and mayonnaise together. Combine all the salad ingredients thoroughly and chill before serving.

Any other flavourful vegetarian hard cheeses work well here too.

113 Golden beetroot salad

Serves 4

Ingredients
- 1 golden beetroot
- 3 broccoli stems
- 2 carrots
- 85 g cashew nuts
- 85 golden sultanas

For the dressing
- 1 shallot
- 1 garlic cove
- Juice ½ lemon
- 2 tablespoons maple syrup
- 2 tablespoons Dijon mustard
- 125 ml olive oil

Preparation
Peel the beetroot, broccoli stems and carrots and cut into matchsticks. Put the cashew nuts into a heavy-bottomed saucepan and dry-roast for around four minutes, stirring frequently until they begin to colour. Turn them onto a plate to stop them from cooking further.

To make the dressing, peel and chop the shallot and garlic and put them in a food processor with the other dressing ingredients. Whiz to combine. Toss all the ingredients together in a serving bowl and serve immediately.

Five ways with zucchini

114

Battered

Slice courgettes, dip them in a light beer batter and fry for a very special summer treat. To make the batter, whisk together 115 g plain flour, 25 g cornflour, 150 ml light beer and 150 ml soda water. Dust the battered slices with hot paprika and serve with a sour cream and chive dip.

115

Crispy kofta

Mix grated courgette with gram (chickpea) flour and garam masala to make a stiff paste, then fry small balls until crisp and golden. Serve as finger food with a mango chutney dip.

116

Stuffed trio

Your favourite pepper stuffing can also be used in a courgette. Halve lengthways, scoop out the seeds, stuff and bake under foil in a medium-heat oven for 25 minutes, until tender. Try serving a pretty trio of stuffed courgette, tomato and pepper.

117

Griddled slices

Thinly slice courgette lengthways, brush with olive oil and place in a hot griddle pan. Avoid moving them until you turn them – this way you'll get clear stripes on the flesh.

118

Raw glory

Raw-food enthusiasts use fine strips of courgette like pasta, serving it with a spicy raw tomato sauce. Use a potato peeler or invest in a spiraliser to get really long, thin courgette ribbons.

119 Mushrooms stuffed with bulgur wheat

Serves 4

Ingredients
- 6 large Portobello mushrooms (or other large flat mushrooms)
- 1 small onion
- ½ green pepper
- 1 tablespoon olive oil
- 1 teaspoon wholegrain mustard
- 55 g cracked bulgur wheat
- Salt and freshly ground black pepper

Preparation
Preheat the oven to 190°C.

Wipe the mushrooms and remove and discard the stalks. Peel and finely chop the onion. Finely chop the green pepper.

Heat the oil and gently fry the onion and green pepper for two minutes, then stir in the mustard, bulgur wheat, chopped mushroom stalks and 150 ml of water. Bring to the boil, then turn down the heat and simmer, covered, for 10 minutes or until the bulgur wheat has absorbed all the water. Season generously with salt and pepper.

Put the mushrooms upside down in a lightly greased baking dish and divide the filling between them. Drizzle with a little extra olive oil and cook for 15 minutes, until heated through.

120 Puy lentil salad with mangetout and broccoli

Serves 4

Ingredients
- 200 g Puy lentils
- 1 litre vegetable stock
- 140 g broccoli
- 140 g mangetout
- 140 g edamame beans

For the dressing
- 1 clove garlic
- 2 tablespoons rapeseed oil
- Juice 1 lemon
- 2 tablespoons soy sauce
- ½ teaspoon red chilli flakes
- 1 tablespoon honey

Preparation
Cook the lentils in the stock for 15 minutes, until tender but not disintegrating. Drain and set aside to cool. Cut the broccoli into small florets. Bring a large saucepan of water to the boil and blanch the broccoli, mangetout and edamame beans for two minutes. Drain and refresh under cold water.

To make the dressing, peel and crush the garlic, and combine with all the remaining ingredients. Mix well. Toss the cooked vegetables, lentils and dressing together and serve chilled.

121 Fruit and nut coleslaw

Serves 4

Ingredients

- 115 g white cabbage
- 2 carrots
- 1 red apple
- 55 g dried apricots
- 3 tablespoons mayonnaise
- 3 tablespoons crème fraîche
- Salt and freshly ground black pepper
- 55 g raisins
- 3 tablespoons pecan pieces

Preparation

Finely shred the cabbage. Peel the carrots, if necessary, and coarsely shred. Finely chop the apple and the apricots. Mix the mayonnaise and crème fraîche together and season well.

Put all the ingredients into a large serving bowl, add the raisins and pecan pieces and mix thoroughly. Serve immediately.

122 Watermelon and feta salad

Serves 4

Ingredients

- 900 g seedless watermelon
- ½ red onion
- 200 g feta cheese
- Handful fresh mint
- Juice ½ lemon
- 4 tablespoons olive oil

Preparation

Cut away the rind of the melon and cut the flesh into bite-sized pieces, removing any seeds. Peel and finely slice the onion. Cut the feta cheese into small cubes. Chop the mint. Mix the lemon juice and olive oil together.

Put the watermelon onto a large serving plate, top with the onion, feta and mint, then pour the dressing over the salad just before serving.

123 Garden salad
Serves 4

Ingredients
- 225 g baby new potatoes
- 140 g green or runner beans
- Few fresh chives
- Few sprigs fresh parsley
- 2 tablespoons plain yogurt
- 2 tablespoons mayonnaise
- 1 tablespoon wholegrain mustard
- Salt and freshly ground black pepper
- 55 g Little Gem lettuce
- 55 g radishes
- 4 spring onions
- 10 cherry tomatoes

Preparation
Cook the potatoes in boiling, salted water until tender, about 10 minutes depending on their size. Trim and chop the beans into short lengths. Add these to the potatoes for the last five minutes of cooking. Drain the beans and potatoes, and refresh them under cold running water, then set aside to drain and cool.

Chop the chives and the parsley. Mix the yogurt, mayonnaise, mustard and chopped herbs together thoroughly. Season with salt and pepper to taste.

Shred the lettuce and slice the radishes finely. Trim and chop the spring onions. Cut the tomatoes into halves or quarters. Mix all the ingredients together in a large bowl and serve immediately.

124 Stuffed tomatoes

Serves 4

Ingredients
- 1 onion
- 3 cloves garlic
- Handful pitted black olives
- 8 large ripe tomatoes
- 1 tablespoon olive oil
- Few sprigs fresh parsley
- 70 g basmati rice
- 60 ml dry white wine
- 125 ml vegetable stock
- Salt and freshly ground black pepper

Preparation
Preheat the oven to 180°C.

Peel and chop the onion, and peel and crush the garlic. Roughly chop the olives. Slice the tops off the tomatoes and set the tops aside for later. Scoop out the flesh and reserve this too. Chop the fresh parsley. Heat the oil in a large saucepan and gently fry the onion and garlic until soft. Stir in the reserved tomato flesh, olives and parsley. Heat through, then stir in the rice, wine and stock. Bring to the boil, reduce to a simmer and cook, covered, for 15 minutes. Season to taste.

Spoon the filling carefully into the tomatoes and put them in a greased, shallow baking dish. Replace the tomato tops and bake for 30 minutes, until the rice is tender and the tomatoes are soft.

Long-grain basmati rice absorbs the moisture in the stuffing without losing its shape or texture. Tomatoes, olives, parsley and garlic are natural partners and this is an attractive way to deliver some traditional rustic flavours.

125 Roasted beetroot with basil

Serves 4

Ingredients
- 6 beetroots
- 6 cloves garlic
- Handful of fresh basil
- Salt and freshly ground black pepper
- 2 tablespoons olive oil

Preparation
Preheat the oven to 180°C.

Peel the beetroots and cut them into quarters. Leave the skin on the garlic, but cut each clove in half lengthways. Leave the basil intact; there is no need to chop it up.

Toss all the ingredients together and wrap in a well-sealed parcel of kitchen foil or a roasting bag. Bake for 40 minutes, until the beetroots are tender.

126 Herb polenta cakes

Makes 12

Ingredients
- 500 ml vegetable stock
- 125 g polenta
- 100 g vegetarian ricotta cheese
- 2 tablespoons chopped fresh herbs: any combination of tarragon, basil, thyme and parsley
- 25 g salted butter

Preparation
Put the stock into a large saucepan and bring to the boil. Gradually beat in the polenta and cook, stirring continuously, for two minutes. Remove from the heat and stir in the cheese and herbs. Transfer to a shallow, greased baking dish and chill for 30 minutes until firm.

When the polenta is firm and cold, turn it out of the dish and use a small round cutter (approximately 8 cm in diameter) to press out the polenta cakes. Gently fry the cakes in the butter for around five minutes, until crisp and golden on both sides.

These are perfect with simply prepared summer vegetables or asparagus spears.

127 Roasted summer vegetables

Serves 4

Ingredients
- 3 courgettes
- 1 small aubergine
- 3 red, orange or yellow peppers
- 1 red onion
- 4 cloves garlic
- 3 tablespoons olive oil
- 2 teaspoons fennel seeds

Preparation
Preheat the oven to 220°C.

Trim and slice the courgettes, aubergine and peppers. Peel and slice the onion. Leave the garlic skin intact. Put the vegetables into a large mixing bowl and toss with the olive oil and fennel seeds. Spread out on a baking tray and cook for 30 minutes, stirring occasionally, until the vegetables are soft and browning.

Serve hot, advising your diners to squeeze the soft roast garlic flesh out of the crisp skins, carefully mixing it with the rest of the vegetables.

If you want to serve this dish cold, retrieve the garlic and squeeze the soft garlic flesh into a dressing of balsamic vinegar and olive oil. Toss through the dish just before serving.

128 Classic pizza base

Serves 4

Ingredients
- 375 g strong plain flour
- 1 teaspoon salt
- 1 tablespoon sugar
- 7 g dried active yeast
- 2 tablespoons olive oil

Preparation
Preheat the oven to 230°C.

Mix the flour, salt, sugar and yeast together in a large bowl. Stir in the oil and 225 ml of warm water. Turn the mixture onto a floured worktop and knead for five minutes, until smooth and elastic. Divide the dough into four equal pieces and roll each piece into a 15-cm circle. Put on a lightly oiled baking tray and leave in a warm place to rise for 15 minutes. Cover the bases with the toppings of your choice and bake for 10 minutes.

Try topping with Roasted Summer Vegetables (see left), classic tomato sauce and mozzarella, or try something more adventurous such as wild mushrooms and goat's cheese, overleaf.

129 Wild mushroom and tomato pizza

Serves 4

Ingredients
- 1 onion
- 85 g mixed wild mushrooms
- 1 large ripe tomato
- Few sprigs fresh thyme
- 1 tablespoon olive oil
- Salt and freshly ground black pepper
- 85 g crumbly goat's cheese

Preparation

Peel and chop the onion finely. Wipe, trim and slice the mushrooms. Peel, de-seed and slice the tomato. Strip the thyme leaves from their stalks and chop finely. Heat the olive oil in a frying pan and gently fry the onion and mushrooms together until the onions are soft. Stir in the chopped thyme, salt and pepper.

Prepare four small pizza bases (see page 101). Divide the mushroom mixture between the bases and top with the tomato slices and crumbled goat's cheese. Bake according to the pizza base recipe.

A mixture of interesting mushrooms gives new interest and texture to this international favourite. Don't overcook the mushrooms; remember they'll be finished in the oven.

130 Courgette and paprika fritters

Serves 4

Ingredients
- 3 courgettes
- 85 g plain flour
- 1 teaspoon paprika
- 1 teaspoon ground cumin
- Pinch salt
- Vegetable oil for frying

Preparation
Trim and slice the courgettes. Mix together the flour, spices and salt and spread over a plate.

Heat the oil in a large frying pan. Dip the courgettes into the spiced flour, coating both sides, and then fry gently for up to four minutes, until golden and crisp.

131 Stuffed Ramiro peppers

Serves 4

Ingredients
- 85 g wholewheat couscous
- Handful fresh coriander
- Juice 1 lemon
- 115 g cherry tomatoes
- Salt and freshly ground black pepper
- 4 Ramiro peppers

Preparation
Preheat the oven to 180°C.

Spread the couscous out in a large shallow dish and just cover with boiling water. Allow to sit for 15 minutes until the water is absorbed, then fluff gently with a fork. Chop the coriander and mix into the couscous with the lemon juice. Cut the tomatoes into quarters and mix into the couscous. Season to taste with salt and pepper.

Cut the peppers in half lengthways and remove the seeds. Carefully fill each half with the couscous mixture, and put on a greased baking tray. Cook for 20 minutes, until the peppers are soft and the couscous is heated through.

132 Fritto misto

Serves 4

Ingredients

- 900 g mixed summer vegetables:
  baby carrots, baby courgettes,
  sugar snap peas, mangetout,
  peppers, spring onions, onions
- 1 lemon
- 140 g plain flour
- 1 tablespoon olive oil
- 2 medium egg whites
- Rapeseed oil, for frying

Preparation

Trim the vegetables, peel if necessary, and chop into bite-sized pieces. Cut the lemon into wedges.

Put the flour into a large mixing bowl and make a well in the centre. Gradually mix in the olive oil along with sufficient warm water to make a smooth, thin batter. Beat the egg whites to stiff peaks and fold them into the mixture.

Fill a large, deep frying pan or wok to a depth of 2.5 cm with rapeseed oil. Dip the vegetables into the batter and shallow fry in small batches until crisp and golden. Serve immediately with lemon wedges.

This is a lovely summery starter or light main dish using the season's freshest baby vegetables. Don't overwhelm them with the batter – a little is enough.

133 Brazil nut burgers

Serves 4

Ingredients

- 85 g Brazil nuts
- 1 onion
- 1 carrot
- 1 medium egg
- 1 tablespoon rapeseed oil
- 115 g breadcrumbs
- 2 tablespoons sun-dried
  tomato paste
- 1 teaspoon dried thyme
- Salt and freshly ground black pepper

Preparation

Put the nuts into a food processor and process to a powder. Peel and finely chop the onion. Peel and grate the carrots. Beat the egg.

Heat the oil in a frying pan and gently fry the onion until it is soft. Transfer to a mixing bowl and mix in the nuts, breadcrumbs, egg, carrots, tomato paste and thyme. Season to taste with salt and pepper.

Divide the mixture into four equal portions and shape each into a burger. Put on a baking tray lined with baking parchment and brush with a little more oil. Grill, turning gently, until browned on both sides.

Five ways with tomatoes

134
Speedy gratin
For a quick and inexpensive lunch, cover ripe tomatoes and a sprig of rosemary with breadcrumbs, garlic and diced cheese. Drizzle with olive oil and bake at 190°C for 30 minutes.

135
Sun-dried quarters
Make your own sun-dried tomatoes by quartering cherry tomatoes and tossing them in olive oil. Space them out on a baking tray lined with baking parchment and bake for four hours at 110°C – or the lowest temperature your oven offers.

136
Baked on the vine
Simply put a whole stalk of tomatoes on a baking tray and roast at 200°C for 10 minutes, until the tomatoes begin to colour and split. Serve with a simple plate of scrambled eggs on toast and a good twist of fresh black pepper.

137
Italian Caprese salad
Arrange slices of ripe tomato and buffalo mozzarella on a plate. Garnish with torn basil and dress with a splash of balsamic vinegar and olive oil.

138
Shallow-fried
Get the best out of the end-of-season green tomatoes by serving them up Southern style. Slice them, dredge them in seasoned cornmeal and shallow fry on both sides until browned and crisp.

139 Tofu mushroom burgers

Serves 4

V

Ingredients

- 225 g firm tofu
- 225 g fresh breadcrumbs
- 1 onion
- 2 carrots
- 115 g button mushrooms
- 2 cloves garlic
- Few sprigs fresh tarragon
- 2 tablespoons rapeseed oil, plus extra for frying
- 1 teaspoon sun-dried tomato paste
- 1 tablespoon soy sauce
- 1 tablespoon peanut butter

Preparation

Press and drain the tofu and mash it together with the breadcrumbs in a large mixing bowl. Peel and finely chop the onion. Peel and grate the carrots. Wipe and slice the mushrooms. Peel and crush the garlic. Chop the tarragon.

Heat the oil in a large frying pan and gently fry the onion, mushrooms, carrots and garlic until the onions are soft and translucent. Add the cooked vegetables to the tofu mixture, along with the tomato paste, soy sauce, peanut butter and tarragon. Mix together thoroughly. Shape into eight small burgers and shallow fry until browned and crisp on both sides.

Be sure to buy firm tofu for these burgers. The best way to mix the ingredients together is to use your hands – if you want to involve children with cooking, this is the perfect job for them!

140 Summer vegetable ketchup

Serves 4

Ingredients

- 2 onions
- 2 sticks celery
- 3 carrots
- 3 cloves garlic
- Sprig fresh sage
- Sprig fresh rosemary
- 4 tablespoons olive oil
- 1 bay leaf
- 1.5 kg ripe tomatoes
- 70 g brown sugar
- 125 ml red wine vinegar
- 1 teaspoon salt
- 1 teaspoon cayenne pepper

Preparation

Peel and finely chop the onion. Trim and finely chop the celery and the carrots. Peel and crush the garlic. Strip the sage and rosemary from their stalks and chop finely.

Heat the olive oil in a large saucepan and gently fry the onion, celery and carrots until soft. Add the garlic and bay leaf, and cook for a further minute or two. Remove the bay leaf and put the mixture into a food processor. Blend until smooth.

Pour boiling water into a bowl and skin the tomatoes by plunging them first into the hot water and then into a bowl of cold water. The skins should split and slide off easily. Put half of the skinned tomatoes into the food processor and process until smooth. Return to the pan with the rest of the tomatoes and the other ingredients. Bring to the boil and then simmer, covered, for 30 minutes. Pour into sterilised jars, seal and use within three months.

141 Green pepper soufflé omelette

Serves 4

Ingredients

- ½ onion
- 1 green pepper
- 2 medium eggs
- 100 g vegetarian ricotta cheese
- Freshly ground black pepper
- 2 teaspoons rapeseed oil

Preparation

Peel and finely chop the onion. De-seed and finely chop the pepper. Separate the eggs. Beat the egg yolks with the ricotta and 1 tablespoon of water until smooth and season to taste with black pepper. Beat the egg whites to stiff peaks and gently fold into the ricotta with the onion and pepper.

Heat the oil in a small, non-stick frying pan and cook the mixture gently for up to six minutes, until golden brown on the bottom. Put the frying pan under a preheated grill to brown the top. Use a spatula to loosen the omelette from the pan and serve immediately.

Ricotta cheese is not always suitable for vegetarians – check the label to see if it has been made with animal rennet.

142 Potato and spring onion frittata

Serves 4

Ingredients

- 350 g new potatoes
- 6 spring onions
- Handful fresh basil
- 4 medium eggs
- 2 tablespoons olive oil
- Salt and freshly ground black pepper

Preparation

Cook the potatoes in a pan of boiling salted water until tender and cooked through, about 10 minutes. Drain and, when cool enough to handle, slice thickly. Trim and chop the spring onions. Chop the basil. Beat the eggs.

Heat the oil in a small, deep, non-stick frying pan and fry the sliced potatoes for up to 10 minutes, until browned and crisp. Mix the eggs together with the spring onions, basil and seasoning. Pour the eggs into the frying pan on top of the potatoes and stir quickly to mix through. Cook the frittata on a low heat until it is almost completely set.

Preheat the grill, then put the frying pan under the grill for three minutes to finish the cooking. Eat hot or cold.

If your frying pan doesn't have a metal handle, don't put it under the grill. Instead, turn the frittata by taking the pan off the heat, covering it with a plate and carefully turning the pan and plate over. It's best to wear an oven glove, as there may be some hot oil spillage! Then slide the frittata from the plate back into the pan and continue to cook on the other side for a further three minutes.

143 Courgette and tomato galette

Serves 4

Ingredients

- 3 courgettes
- 8 ripe tomatoes
- 4 cloves garlic
- 4 tablespoons rapeseed oil
- 1 teaspoon paprika
- 1 tablespoon sun-dried tomato paste
- 1 medium egg
- 600 g cooked brown rice
- 1 tablespoon soy sauce
- Salt and freshly ground black pepper
- Oil, for greasing and drizzling

Preparation

Preheat the oven to 200°C.

Grease and line a 28-cm springform cake tin with baking parchment.

Trim and thinly slice the courgette. Roughly chop the tomatoes. Peel and crush the garlic. Heat the oil in a large saucepan or wok and stir-fry the courgette for up to five minutes, until beginning to brown. Add the garlic, tomatoes, paprika and tomato paste. Cook on a high heat for two minutes, then reduce the heat and simmer, covered, for 10 minutes. Season to taste with salt and pepper.

Beat the egg. Mix the cooked rice with 2 tablespoons of the courgette mixture, the egg and the soy sauce. Put half the rice mixture into the prepared pan, press down firmly with the back of the spoon and smooth the top. Cover with the courgette and tomato mixture.

Carefully spoon the rest of the rice on top, and gently smooth it over the top of the galette.

Drizzle over a little more oil and bake for 25 minutes, until golden and crisp. Allow to rest for five minutes before releasing the pan and slicing. Serve hot or cold.

144 Cheese gougères
Serves 4

Ingredients
* 115 g Cheddar cheese
* 115 g salted butter
* ½ teaspoon salt
* 140 g plain flour
* 4 medium eggs

Preparation
Preheat the oven to 220°C.

Grate the cheese. Put the butter and salt into a pan with 250 ml of water. Bring to the boil, then reduce the heat to low and add the flour in a single batch. Stir rapidly and continuously with a wooden spoon as the mixture comes together. Cook for up to three minutes, until the mixture forms a smooth ball. Take the pan off the heat and allow it cool for a few minutes.

Beat the eggs. Add them to the warm dough one at a time, beating thoroughly to incorporate. Finally, mix in the grated cheese. Put small spoonfuls of the mixture onto a baking tray lined with baking parchment, leaving room between each spoonful for the pastry to puff up. Bake for 10 minutes, turn the heat down to 180°C and cook for a further 15 minutes, until the pastries are cooked through and golden.

Serve warm or cold as canapés, or make a meal by placing five or six balls in a shallow bowl with a simple tomato or pasta sauce.

Choux pastry, or pâte à choux, is a French favourite – classically, it is used to make sweet profiteroles but it can be used in savoury dishes too. These buns should be crisp and golden on the outside, and light and fluffy within.

145 Sweet-and-sour summer vegetables

Serves 4

Ingredients

- 175 g new potatoes
- 85 g each of carrots, courgettes and mushrooms
- ½ medium red pepper
- ¼ large apple
- 55 g water chestnuts
- 300 ml vegetable stock
- 85 g tinned chopped tomatoes

For the sauce

- 115 g onions
- 1 clove garlic
- 1 tablespoon rapeseed oil
- 1 tablespoon tomato purée
- 1 tablespoon soy sauce
- 2 tablespoons white wine vinegar
- 1 teaspoon ground ginger
- 2 teaspoons soft brown sugar
- Salt and freshly ground black pepper
- 2 teaspoons arrowroot powder

Preparation

Peel the potatoes and chop into small pieces. Peel the carrots and slice finely. Trim and slice the courgettes. Slice the mushrooms. De-seed and slice the pepper. Core and slice the apple. Slice the water chestnuts.

Put the potatoes, carrots, pepper and apple into a large saucepan. Add the stock – reserving 4 tablespoons. Cook until tender, drain and set aside. Put 2 tablespoons of the reserved stock into a large frying pan and cook the remaining vegetables for five minutes, until tender.

To make the sauce, peel and finely chop the onions and peel and crush the garlic. Warm the oil in a large saucepan and fry the onions until soft. Stir in the garlic. Add the rest of the ingredients, except for the arrowroot. Mix this with the last of the stock and add to the sauce. Add the vegetables and bring to the boil. Reduce the heat and simmer for five minutes until the sauce is glossy.

146 Grilled corncobs with garlic sauce

Serves 4

Ingredients
• 4 whole corncobs, husks still on

For the sauce
• 4 cloves garlic
• 55 g fresh white breadcrumbs
• 55 g ground almonds
• Juice 1 lemon
• 150 ml olive oil
• Salt and freshly ground black pepper

Preparation
Carefully fold back the leaves of each corncob to reveal the silk strings inside. Pull out the silks and fold the leaves back into place. Put the whole corncobs onto a grill and cook for around 40 minutes, turning occasionally, until the kernels are soft and juicy, and come away from the cob easily.

Peel and crush the garlic. Put the breadcrumbs into a small bowl, cover with water and leave to soak for five minutes. Drain off the water and squeeze the breadcrumbs together to remove as much water as you can. Put the soaked bread into a blender with the ground almonds, garlic and lemon juice. Blend to a smooth paste, then gradually pour in the olive oil, keeping the motor running, to make a sauce with the consistency of mayonnaise. Season to taste. When the corn is ready, pull back the leaves and smear the garlic sauce over the exposed kernels before eating.

147 Basque-style piperade

Serves 4

Ingredients

- 4 peppers (a mixture of colours)
- 2 red onions
- 2 cloves garlic
- 5 tomatoes
- 2 tablespoons olive oil
- Salt and freshly ground black pepper
- 4 medium eggs
- 4 tablespoons milk

Preparation

De-seed and slice the peppers. Peel and slice the onions. Peel and crush the garlic. Peel and slice the tomatoes.

Heat the oil in a large, heavy-bottomed saucepan and gently fry the onions, peppers and garlic for a minute. Turn the heat to a minimum, cover the pan and allow the vegetables to sweat for five minutes, stirring occasionally, until the peppers are soft. Season with salt and pepper.

Beat the eggs and milk together, then stir into the hot vegetables, keeping the pan on a medium heat. Stir continuously until the egg is cooked and well mixed with the vegetables. Serve immediately.

This hearty rustic dish has its roots in the Basque country between France and Spain. Try it for breakfast as well as lunch and dinner!

148 Apple cider-baked baby potatoes

Serves 4

Ingredients

- 450 g new potatoes
- 4 shallots
- 2 tart apples
- 100 g Lancashire cheese
- 150 ml dry apple cider

Preparation

Preheat the oven to 190°C.

Scrub the potatoes if necessary and slice them approximately 0.5-cm thick. Peel and finely slice the shallots. Core and thinly slice the apples. Grate the cheese.

Layer the potatoes, shallots, apples and cheese into a lightly greased baking dish, ending with a layer of cheese. Pour the cider over the dish, cover with kitchen foil and bake for one hour, until the potatoes and apples are cooked through and tender.

149 Baked baby potatoes in parchment parcels

V

Serves 4

Ingredients
- 900 g baby new potatoes
- 4 tablespoons olive oil
- 4 sprigs of herbs: any combination of sage, rosemary and thyme
- 4 cloves garlic
- Salt and freshly ground black pepper

Preparation
Preheat the oven to 200°C.

Clean the potatoes but leave the skins on. Put them into a large bowl and toss with the oil, whole herb sprigs, unpeeled garlic cloves and salt and pepper.

Put the mixed ingredients on a large sheet of baking parchment and fold up the edges to make a parcel. Transfer to a baking tray and cook for 45 minutes, until the potatoes are tender.

150 Barbecued sweet potato with aioli

Serves 4

Ingredients
- 450 g sweet potatoes
- 4 tablespoons olive oil

For the aioli
- 5 cloves garlic
- 2 egg yolks
- Juice 1 lemon
- 300 ml olive oil
- Salt and freshly ground black pepper

Preparation
Preheat grill. Peel the sweet potatoes and cut into slices about 0.5-cm thick. Brush with olive oil and grill for about five minutes on each side until tender.

To make the aioli, peel and crush the garlic. Put it into a blender with the egg yolks and half of the lemon juice. Blend briefly to mix the ingredients together, then, with the motor running, gradually pour in the olive oil to make a thick mayonnaise. Season to taste with salt and pepper, and more lemon juice if you like. Serve the grilled sweet potato slices hot with the aioli on the side.

151 Marinated vegetable kebabs

Serves 4

Ingredients
- 1 red pepper
- 1 yellow pepper
- 2 courgettes
- 1 red onion
- 6 button mushrooms

For the marinade
- 300 ml vegetable oil
- Juice of 1 lemon
- 2 bay leaves
- 4 tablespoons fresh chopped herbs:
  any combination of parsley, thyme,
  basil, mint and oregano
- 2 cloves garlic
- 1 teaspoon ground cumin
- ½ teaspoon cayenne pepper

Preparation

Preheat grill. Cut the peppers into pieces approximately
2.5-cm square. Slice the courgette into pieces approximately
2.5-cm thick. Peel the onion and cut into eighths. Cut the
mushrooms in half.

To make the marinade, mix together the oil, lemon juice,
bay leaves, fresh herbs, garlic and spices. Put the prepared
vegetables into a large shallow dish and cover with the
marinade. Cover with a lid and leave to soak for at least
one hour, stirring occasionally.

Divide the marinated vegetables between eight large skewers
and grill or barbecue, turning frequently, for up to 15 minutes,
until cooked through and browned in places.

*Think about how you will thread the cut vegetables onto the
skewer as you prepare them – they should all be roughly the same
size so that they cook evenly. Pieces that are too thin may burn or
fall off the skewer!*

152 Mediterranean vegetable loaf

Serves 4

Ingredients
- 3 red peppers
- 3 yellow peppers
- 5 tablespoons olive oil
- 1 aubergine
- 2 courgettes
- 1 red onion
- Handful basil
- Handful black olives
- 800 g crusty white bread loaf
- 2 tablespoons vegetarian or vegan pesto

Preparation
Preheat the oven to 220°C.

De-seed and slice the peppers, place on a baking tray, toss with 2 tablespoons of olive oil and cook for up to 20 minutes, until soft. Transfer the peppers to a sealable plastic food bag, close and leave to cool. Peel the skins off the peppers and discard. Trim and slice the aubergine and courgettes, and toss with the remaining oil. Griddle in small batches, leaving undisturbed on the hot pan to get clear stripes. Set aside to cool. Peel and finely chop the onion. Chop the herbs and olives.

Slice the loaf in half lengthways and scoop out the soft bread inside to make two crusty shells. Layer the cooked vegetables into the bread shells, dotting each layer with onion, pesto, olives and basil. Sandwich the filled bread halves back together, press together firmly and wrap tightly in cling film. Refrigerate for an hour, then slice carefully to serve.

153 Crunchy stuffed courgettes

Serves 4

Ingredients

- 1 onion
- 3 tomatoes
- 1 red pepper
- 200 g cooked chickpeas
- 4 large courgettes
- 1 tablespoon olive oil
- 2 teaspoons dried thyme
- 100 g Cheddar cheese
- 100 g plain yogurt
- ½ teaspoon paprika
- 25 g plain potato crisps

Preparation

Preheat the oven to 200°C.

Peel and finely chop the onion. Skin and chop the tomatoes. De-seed and chop the red pepper. Drain and rinse the chickpeas. Halve the courgettes lengthways and, using a teaspoon, scoop out the flesh, leaving shells about 0.5-cm thick. Reserve the flesh.

Heat the olive oil and gently fry the onion, courgette flesh, pepper, tomatoes, chickpeas and thyme for five minutes, until softened.

Put the courgette shells into a lightly greased baking dish and divide the filling between the shells. Grate the cheese and mix it with the yogurt and paprika. Spoon the cheese mixture over the filled courgettes. Crush the potato crisps and sprinkle them over the dish. Bake for 20 minutes, until heated through and crispy on top.

154 Courgette and herb penne

Serves 4

Ingredients

- 4 courgettes
- 1 clove garlic
- 4 tablespoons olive oil
- 1 bay leaf
- 1 whole, dried red chilli
- Handful basil
- Handful parsley
- 5 spring onions
- 450 g dried penne
- Salt and freshly ground black pepper

Preparation

Trim and slice the courgettes. Peel the garlic, but leave it whole. Warm the olive oil in a large frying pan or wok and gently cook the garlic, bay leaf and chilli until the garlic is golden. Scoop the garlic, bay leaf and chilli out of the oil and discard them. Fry the courgettes in the same oil for about four minutes, until soft but not disintegrating. Roughly chop the basil and parsley, and trim and finely chop the spring onions.

Cook the pasta in boiling salted water, until tender, about nine to 10 minutes, and drain. Add the pasta to the courgettes in the frying pan. Stir in the basil, parsley and spring onions and cook gently for three minutes, until the the dish is heated through. Season to taste with salt and pepper.

Other pasta can be used, but tube-shaped penne holds its shape well and makes a nice textural and visual contrast with the softened vegetables.

155 Twice-cooked summer vegetables

Serves 4

Ingredients
- 1 onion
- 2 cloves garlic
- 2 red peppers
- 2 yellow peppers
- 115 g runner beans
- 1 large potato
- 4 tablespoons olive oil
- Salt and freshly ground black pepper

Preparation

Peel and slice the onion. Peel and crush the garlic. De-seed and slice the peppers. Trim and slice the runner beans into thin strips. Peel the potato and cut into fine matchsticks.

Toss the prepared vegetables together with the olive oil and put into a large flameproof casserole dish. Stir-fry for two minutes, then reduce the heat to minimum, cover and sweat for 15 minutes, until the potatoes are tender. Season to taste with salt and pepper, and serve hot.

Stir-frying the vegetables before sweating them gently means that they will be soft and succulent.

156 Leek and lemon linguine

Serves 4

Ingredients
- 4 leeks
- 2 cloves garlic
- Handful fresh basil
- Handful fresh rocket
- 3 tablespoons olive oil
- 4 tablespoons dry white wine
- 1 lemon
- 300 ml crème fraîche
- 55 g vegetarian Parmesan-style cheese
- 300 g dried linguine
- Salt and freshly ground black pepper

Preparation

Trim and finely slice the leeks. Peel and crush the garlic. Chop the fresh herbs. Zest and juice the lemon. Warm the oil in a large saucepan and gently fry the leeks until soft. Stir in the garlic and cook for a further minute, then add the wine, lemon juice and lemon zest. Cook on a low heat for five minutes. Stir in the crème fraîche and vegetarian Parmesan-style cheese.

Cook the pasta in salted boiling water, until tender. Drain and add to the leeks with the chopped basil and rocket. Stir together and heat through to serve. Season to taste with salt and pepper.

157 Lentils spiced with harissa

Serves 4

V

Ingredients

- 225 g brown lentils
- 1 onion
- 3 cloves garlic
- 1 teaspoon cumin seeds
- 1 cinnamon stick
- 2 tablespoons olive oil
- 1 teaspoon harissa paste
- 1 teaspoon chilli powder, or to taste
- 2 bay leaves
- Salt and freshly ground black pepper

Preparation

Rinse the lentils and put them into a large saucepan. Cover with 600 ml of water, bring to the boil and simmer, covered, for 20 minutes until the lentils are soft but not mushy. Drain the lentils, reserving the cooking water for later.

Peel and finely chop the onion. Peel and crush the garlic. Crush the cumin seeds with the back of a spoon, cracking them just to let the flavour out.

Heat the oil in a large saucepan and gently fry the onion until soft and translucent. Stir in the garlic, the harissa and all the spices. Stir-fry for two minutes, then add the lentils, the bay leaves and 225 ml of the reserved cooking liquid. Simmer, uncovered, on a very low heat for 20 minutes and serve warm.

Harissa is a spicy paste made from puréed red peppers and chillies. Although it originated in Tunisia, it is widely used in Arabic countries. Ingredients vary, but it may include garlic, cumin, coriander, lemon juice and caraway seeds.

158 Summer ratatouille

Serves 4

Ingredients
- 225 g onions
- 2 cloves garlic
- 225 g courgettes
- 2 red peppers
- 225 g marrow
- 1 x 400 g tin chickpeas
- Few sprigs fresh parsley
- 1 vegetable stock cube
- 2 tablespoons olive oil
- 2 x 400 g tins chopped tomatoes
- Salt and freshly ground black pepper

Preparation

Peel and roughly chop the onions. Peel and chop the garlic. Trim and slice the courgettes. De-seed and slice the peppers. Peel the marrow and chop it into bite-sized pieces. Drain and rinse the chickpeas. Finely chop the parsley. Crumble the stock cube to a powder.

In a flameproof casserole dish, fry the onion in the olive oil until soft, then add the garlic and cook for another minute. Add all the other ingredients, cover and simmer on a very low heat for 30 minutes.

This is a traditional stewed vegetable dish from the Provence region of France, which has found its way onto the menu in many other countries. Aubergines and courgettes are key ingredients but other vegetables can be incorporated into the mix, depending on what is abundant at the time.

159 Courgette and tomato tart

Serves 4

Ingredients

- 250 g readymade shortcrust pastry
- 4 courgettes
- 500 g ripe cherry tomatoes
- 115 g Gruyère cheese
- 3 tablespoons vegetarian Parmesan-style cheese
- Handful fresh basil
- 4 medium eggs
- 225 ml crème fraîche
- 90 ml milk
- 1 tablespoon olive oil

Preparation

Preheat the oven to 200°C.

Use the pastry to line a 20-cm pie dish. Refrigerate for 20 minutes, then line with baking parchment, fill with baking beans and bake for 15 minutes. Remove the beans and parchment and return to the oven for a further five minutes. Take the pastry case out of the oven and set aside. Turn the oven temperature down to 180°C.

Trim and thinly slice the courgettes. Halve the tomatoes. Grate the Gruyère cheese and vegetarian Parmesan-style cheese. Chop the basil. Beat the eggs together with the milk and the crème fraîche. Gently fry the courgette slices in the olive oil until beginning to brown, about five minutes.

Put a layer of courgettes (about half of them) into the pastry case and cover with a layer of cherry tomatoes and a layer of Gruyère cheese. Add the rest of the courgettes, the basil and the tomatoes. Mix the remaining Gruyère cheese into the egg mixture and carefully pour this over the top of the vegetables. Sprinkle with vegetarian Parmesan-style cheese and bake for 40 minutes, until set and golden.

Gruyère cheese adds an intriguing flavour to this tart. It has a strong taste, which means you don't have to use a lot to get a great cheesy taste, and it's not as greasy as some other hard cheeses.

160 Sparkling peach sangria

Serves 4

Ingredients
- 70 g brown sugar
- 3 large, ripe peaches
- 500 ml dry white wine
- 90 ml Grand Marnier
- Sparkling white wine, to serve

Preparation
Put the sugar into a small saucepan with 200 ml of water and heat gently, stirring, until the sugar dissolves. Leave to cool.

Peel and stone the peaches, and slice them roughly. Put into the bowl of a food processor with the cooled sugar syrup and process until very smooth. Mix with the dry white wine and Grand Marnier, cover and chill for an hour. Pass the liquid through a muslin-lined sieve, squeezing out as much of the juice as possible. Dilute to taste with sparkling wine.

161 Strawberry smoothie

Serves 4

Ingredients
- 200 g fresh strawberries
- 200 ml plain yogurt
- 100 ml chilled milk
- Vanilla essence, to taste
- Honey, to taste

Preparation
Blend the strawberries, yogurt and milk until smooth. Adjust the flavour to suit your taste with vanilla essence and honey.

162 Pink lemonade
Serves 4

Ingredients
- 2 lemons
- 300 g caster sugar
- 450 g fresh raspberries
- Sparkling mineral water and ice
- Fresh mint sprigs, to garnish

Preparation
Slice the lemons and put them into a large saucepan with the sugar and raspberries.

Add 350 ml of water and bring to the boil. Make sure the sugar is dissolved, then remove from the heat and leave to cool. Press through a sieve to make a cordial that can be stored, refrigerated, for one week.

To serve, mix with sparkling water and ice, then top with a sprig of fresh mint.

163 Iced green tea
Serves 4

Ingredients
- Small handful fresh mint
- 3 green teabags
- 2 tablespoons runny honey

Preparation
Finely chop the mint. Steep all the ingredients in 900 ml of boiling water for five minutes, then remove the teabags and chill thoroughly before serving.

Make an alcoholic version by adding Japanese sake according to your own taste.

164 Egg-free carrot cake

Serves 4

Ingredients
- 225 g carrots
- 225 g self-raising flour
- 1 tablespoon cinnamon
- 1 teaspoon nutmeg
- 115 g unsalted butter
- 115 g honey
- 115 g sugar

Preparation

Preheat the oven to 170°C. Grease a large, round springform cake tin.

Peel and grate the carrots. Sift the flour and spices together in a large mixing bowl. Melt the butter in a small saucepan, add the honey and sugar and stir over a gentle heat until the sugar is dissolved. Pour the sugar and butter mixture into the spiced flour, add the carrots and mix well.

Spoon the mixture into the prepared pan and bake for around 75 minutes, until a skewer inserted into the centre of the cake comes out clean. Allow the cake cool in the tin for 10 minutes before turning out. Decorate with icing sugar and tiny carrot decorations if available.

The secret to success is the long, slow bake for this cake – keep the oven temperature low and be patient! Vegans can substitute maple syrup for the honey and vegan margarine for butter in this recipe. Carrot decorations can often be found in the home baking section of supermarkets, or in specialist kitchenware shops.

165 Vegan lemon-and-lime cheesecake

Serves 6

Ingredients

- 1 lemon
- 1 lime
- 350 g digestive biscuits
- 175 g vegan margarine
- 4 tablespoons agave nectar
- 50 g cornlour
- 400 g silken tofu

Preparation

Zest and juice the lemon and the lime. Crush the biscuits into fine crumbs. Melt the margarine in a small saucepan and mix with the biscuit crumbs. Press the mixture into the base of a 20-cm springform tin, using the back of a spoon to smooth it into a firm crust. Leave to cool.

In a small saucepan, mix the agave nectar with 450 ml of water and blend in the cornflour. Gradually heat to boiling point, beating continuously to prevent any lumps from forming. Once boiling point is reached, reduce the heat and continue to stir until the mixture thickens.

Combine the thickened syrup mixture with the silken tofu and fruit zest and juice and beat until smooth. Spoon over the prepared base, smooth the top and chill for two hours before serving.

166 Melon and ginger cream

Serves 4

Ingredients

- 1 Charentais melon
- 4 pieces preserved stem ginger
- 150 ml whipping cream
- 225 g Greek yogurt
- 4 brandy snaps

Preparation

Cut the melon in half and scoop out the seeds. Cut away the skin and chop the flesh into small pieces. Chop the ginger very finely. Beat the cream lightly and then mix it with the yogurt, melon and half of the ginger. Spoon into four serving dishes and top with the remaining ginger. Chill for 30 minutes, and then serve each portion with a ginger snap.

167 Strawberry crush

Serves 4

Ingredients

- 400 g quark (skimmed milk soft cheese) or light cream cheese
- 1 tablespoon caster sugar
- Juice 1 lemon
- 400 g hulled strawberries
- Sprig fresh mint

Preparation

Put the quark, sugar and lemon juice into a large bowl and mix well. Put the strawberries into another bowl and crush them with the back of a fork, so that they are broken up but not completely mashed. Stir the fruit and quark together and spoon into four serving dishes. Chill and garnish with fresh mint to serve.

168 Cherry almond granola

Serves 4

Ingredients

- 300 g rolled oats
- 2 tablespoons pumpkin seeds
- 2 tablespoons sunflower seeds
- 2 tablespoons sesame seeds
- 200 g flaked almonds
- 1 teaspoon almond essence
- 125 ml maple syrup
- 2 tablespoons rapeseed oil
- 100 g dried cherries

Preparation

Preheat the oven to 150°C.

Mix all the ingredients together except the dried cherries. Spread the mixture over a baking tray lined with baking parchment and bake for 15 minutes. Stir up the mixture, adding in the dried cherries, and return to the oven for up to 15 more minutes, until golden. Tip onto a cold baking tray to cool – it will crisp up more. Store in an airtight container for up to one month.

169 Yogurt and strawberry tart

Serves 8

Ingredients
- 85 g unsalted butter
- 175 g plain flour
- 1 tablespoon icing sugar
- 1 medium egg yolk
- Sprig fresh mint

For the filling
- 900 g plain yogurt
- 225 g caster sugar
- 1 teaspoon vanilla essence
- 175 g fresh hulled strawberries

Preparation

The night before, line a large sieve with several sheets of kitchen towel and place it over a large bowl. Put the yogurt into the sieve and leave it overnight in the refrigerator to drain.

To make the pastry, cut the butter into small pieces and rub into the flour with your fingertips. Stir in the icing sugar and the egg yolk. Mix well, then gradually add cold water, a splash at a time, until the dough comes together and is soft but not sticky. Gather the pastry into a ball, wrap in a plastic bag and chill for about 20 minutes.

Preheat the oven to 190°C. Roll out the pastry thinly and line a 20- to 23-cm tart dish. Prick the base and set aside for 20 minutes, then line the base with baking parchment and fill with baking beans. Bake for 15 minutes, remove the beans and parchment and return to the oven for five more minutes. Set aside to cool.

Mix the thickened yogurt with the sugar and vanilla essence. Arrange the strawberries in the pastry case, spoon the yogurt mixture on top and smooth it out. Chill for two hours before serving, and garnish with a little finely chopped fresh mint.

This is a smooth and refreshing tart, perfect for a warm outdoor dinner party or an afternoon tea. Straining the yogurt is important because it will make the filling firmer and dryer.

170 Crème pâtissière

Serves 4

Ingredients

- 1 large egg plus 1 egg yolk
- 55g caster sugar
- 25g plain flour
- 300 ml milk
- Few drops vanilla essence

Preparation

Beat the egg and egg yolk with the sugar, then gradually beat in the flour and milk. Transfer the mixture to a small saucepan and bring to the boil, whisking continuously. Simmer for about three minutes, then remove from the heat and stir in the vanilla essence. Pour the mixture into a shallow dish to cool, and stir occasionally to prevent a skin from forming.

Crème pâtissière is a useful addition to any cook's repertoire. This recipe can be used as a filling for fruit tarts, eclairs or cakes.

171 Summer fruit tart

Serves 6

Ingredients

- 100 g apricot jam
- 1 sweet pastry case (see page 146)
- 1 recipe crème pâtissière (see left)
- 600 g mixed summer fruits: strawberries, raspberries, blueberries, kiwi fruit, mandarin orange segments

Preparation

Put the jam into a small saucepan with 1 tablespoon of water and heat gently, stirring, to make a syrup. Use a pastry brush to brush the base of the pastry case with the syrup and leave to cool – this will help to keep the base of the tart crisp. Fill the tart with crème pâtissière and cover with a decorative arrangement of your chosen fruit. Brush with the remaining jam syrup and serve at room temperature.

172 Blackberry fool

Serves 4

Ingredients
- 225 g blackberries
- 2 tablespoons runny honey
- 2 tablespoons crème fraîche
- 125 ml thick plain yogurt

Preparation
Put the blackberries into a food processor and blend until liquidised. Pass the mixture through a sieve and discard the seeds. Sweeten the blackberry pulp with the honey. Mix the crème fraîche into the yogurt. Gently swirl the blackberry mixture into the yogurt. Serve chilled.

173 Green tea and orange compote

Serves 4

Ingredients
- 3 green teabags
- Zest 1 unwaxed orange
- 2 tablespoons runny honey
- 450 g mixed dried fruit: apricots, sultanas, figs, pears, raisins, apples

Preparation
Cut any large pieces of fruit into bite-sized pieces. Steep the teabags in 600 ml of boiling water for five minutes, then squeeze the teabags and discard them. Put the tea into a large saucepan and add the orange zest and honey. Warm gently to dissolve the honey and mix well, then stir in the mixed fruit and simmer for 15 minutes. Leave to cool and store refrigerated for up to one week.

174 White chocolate and hazelnut soufflé

Serves 4

Ingredients
- 4 medium eggs
- 115 g plain flour
- 175 ml milk
- 175 g caster sugar
- 115 g white chocolate
- 55 g toasted hazelnuts

For the soufflé moulds
- 25 g unsalted butter
- 25 g caster sugar

Preparation
Preheat the oven to 170°C.

Separate the eggs into yolks and whites. In a small saucepan, mix the yolks with the flour, milk and sugar and heat gently, stirring constantly, until the mixture thickens. Melt the white chocolate in a small heatproof bowl over a pan of hot water and then mix into the flour mixture. Leave to cool. Put the toasted hazelnuts into a food processor and process to a powder.

Melt the butter and brush liberally onto the insides of four individual soufflé moulds. Spoon a little caster sugar into each mould and tip it so that the sugar sticks to the butter, covering the surface. Tap out any excess.

Fold the ground nuts into the chocolate mixture. Beat the egg whites to stiff peaks and fold them very gently into the chocolate mixture. Spoon the mixture into the moulds and bake for 18 minutes until well risen and just firm. Serve immediately, as they will start to sink as soon as you take them out of the oven.

Since the French invented soufflés, it seems that the whole world has been experimenting with sweet and savoury variations! These elegant individual soufflés have a delicious nutty flavour.

175 Coconut cake
Serves 8

Ingredients
- 200 g creamed coconut
- 3 tablespoons rapeseed oil
- 200 g cream cheese
- 200 g granulated sugar
- 3 tablespoons rose water
- 1 teaspoon vanilla essence
- 6 medium eggs
- 375 g plain flour
- 2 tablespoons ground almonds
- 200 g desiccated coconut

Preparation
Preheat the oven to 170°C. Grease and line a deep 20-cm round cake tin.

Grate the creamed coconut and melt it gently in a pan or in the microwave. Stir in the rapeseed oil and set aside to cool. Beat the cream cheese and sugar together, then mix in the creamed coconut and rapeseed oil mixture, rose water, vanilla essence and eggs. Beat the mixture until fluffy, and then fold in the flour, ground almonds and desiccated coconut.

Spoon into the prepared tin and bake for approximately one hour until a skewer inserted into the centre of the cake comes out clean. Turn out onto a cooling rack and leave to cool before slicing.

Creamed coconut is made from the finely shredded, dehydrated flesh of coconuts. It is usually sold in blocks, and is different from coconut cream, which is like coconut milk but much thicker and richer.

176 Vegan coconut panna cotta
Serves 4

Ingredients
- 350 ml coconut milk
- 4 tablespoons sugar
- 1 tablespoon agar agar flakes
- 125 ml plain or vanilla soya yogurt
- 1 teaspoon vanilla essence
  (omit if using vanilla yogurt)

Preparation
Pour the coconut milk and sugar into a small saucepan and beat in the agar agar flakes. Allow to stand for five minutes, then heat and simmer for five minutes, stirring constantly. Remove the mixture from the heat and push it through a fine sieve. Mix in the yogurt and vanilla essence and pour into four ramekins. Chill for at least two hours before turning out to serve.

Five ways with strawberries

177
Floral accents

Make a simple dish of fresh strawberries into a special event by serving with a home-made sugar syrup flavoured with lavender flowers, geranium leaves, mint, elderflowers or orange zest.

178
Summer pudding

This dessert has a long history, and that's because it's perfect for using up a glut of fresh fruit and some bread. Line a pudding dish with sliced bread and fill with ripe strawberries. Cover with bread and chill. Turn out onto a vintage plate.

179
Dairy delight

Gently crush ripe strawberries, swirl into some whipped cream, Greek yogurt or crème fraîche and chill to serve.

180
Flavour enhancers

The sweet, tart flavour of strawberries are complemented by black pepper and balsamic vinegar. It sounds wrong, but try drizzling a little balsamic syrup over a bowl of strawberries, or surprise guests by offering a twist of black pepper at the table.

181
Quick strawberry sauce

Cook strawberries with a splash of orange juice, and sugar to taste, until they are soft but not disintegrating. Serve cold with yogurt or ice cream.

182 Strawberry and elderflower tart

Serves 6

Ingredients
- 85 g unsalted butter
- 175 g plain flour
- 1 tablespoon icing sugar
- 1 medium egg yolk

For the filling
- 575 g strawberries
- 2 tablespoons elderflower cordial
- 85 g caster sugar
- 2 tablespoons cornflour

Preparation

To make the sweet pastry case, cut the butter into small pieces and rub into the flour with your fingertips. Stir in the icing sugar and the egg yolk. Mix well, then gradually add cold water, a splash at a time, until the dough comes together and is soft but not sticky. Gather into a ball, wrap in a plastic food bag and chill for 20 minutes.

Preheat the oven to 190°C. Roll the pastry out thinly and line a 20- to 23-cm fluted pie dish. Prick the shell and set aside to rest for a further 20 minutes. Line the shell with baking parchment and fill with baking beans. Bake for 15 minutes, remove the beans and parchment and return to the oven for five more minutes. Set aside.

Put 200 g of the strawberries into a food processor and process until smooth. Pour into a saucepan and mix in the cordial and sugar. Mix the cornflour with a little water and then stir into the fruit with 150 ml more water. Bring to the boil, stirring as the mixture thickens. Remove from the heat and leave to cool.

Mix the remaining strawberries into the mixture and then pour into the pastry shell. Chill well before serving.

Strawberries and elderflowers together are the very essence of summer! Stirring fresh strawberries into the glossy sauce adds texture and an extra layer of flavour to this dish.

183 New York cheesecake

Serves 4

Ingredients

- 115 g unsalted butter
- 150 g digestive biscuits
- 700 g cream cheese
- 200 g caster sugar
- 2 teaspoons vanilla essence
- 4 medium eggs

For the topping

- 475 ml sour cream
- 2 tablespoons caster sugar
- ½ teaspoon vanilla essence

Preparation

Preheat the oven to 180°C.

Melt the butter in a small saucepan. Finely crush the digestive biscuits. Mix the biscuit crumbs with the melted butter and press the mixture into the bottom of a 25-cm springform tin, using the back of a spoon to smooth it out and pressing the base into place firmly.

Mix the cream cheese with the sugar and vanilla essence. Beat the eggs and gradually add them to the cream cheese, without over-beating the mixture. Spoon into the tin, smooth the top and bake for 30 minutes.

To make the topping, mix the sour cream, sugar and vanilla essence together. After the cheesecake has baked for 30 minutes, take it out of the oven, pour the topping over the top and return it to the oven to bake for a further 10 minutes. Leave to cool and chill completely before removing from the tin and serving.

184 Valencia orange tart

Serves 6–8

Ingredients

- 125 g plain flour
- 25 g unsweetened cocoa powder
- 55 g sugar
- ¼ teaspoon salt
- 115 g cold, unsalted butter, cut into small cubes
- 1 large egg

For the filling

- 4 medium oranges
- 65 g cornflour
- 250 g caster sugar
- 6 medium egg yolks

For the topping

- 600 ml fresh orange juice
- 200 g sugar, plus more for caramelising the tart
- 1 tablespoon grated orange zest
- 4 to 5 thin-skinned oranges, scrubbed well
- Orange marmalade

Preparation

Preheat the oven to 180°C. Blend the dry ingredients in a food processor, add the butter and pulse to create small pebbles. Mix the egg yolk with a little water and add to the machine while running. Pulse in short bursts until the mixture is crumbly, then tip onto cling film and gather together. Chill for 30 minutes.

Roll the dough out and press it into an 28-cm tart tin with removable base. Chill in the tin for at least 30 minutes. Prick the bottom of the crust with a fork and bake for 12 minutes, rotating halfway through. Remove and leave to cool.

To make the filling, juice and zest the orange, place into a bowl and stir in the cornflour until smooth. Bring 475 ml of water to the boil in a large saucepan and add the cornflour mixture. Whisk until thick and glossy, and remove from the heat. Put the egg yolks and sugar into a medium-sized bowl and beat them together until well combined. Stir the egg mixture into the filling, return the pan to the heat and whisk until the eggs are cooked and the mixture becomes very thick. Allow to cool, then spoon into the pastry case.

To make the topping, mix the juice, sugar and zest in a wide pan and bring to a simmer over medium-high heat, stirring frequently. Slice the oranges about 3-mm thick and add to the juice. Simmer, partially covered, for about 15 minutes. Let the oranges cool, then drain, discard the liquid and pat the slices dry with kitchen towel.

Turn up the oven to 190°C. Spread the marmalade on top of the filling and lay on the orange slices, overlapping them slightly. Bake for 30 minutes, until the oranges are very soft and lightly browned.

Autumn

Soups, salads and starters

Mains and sides

Drinks and sweets

Fresh in Season ...

Pumpkins and squashes

Winter squashes should be firm – a few blemishes on the skin don't really matter unless you're serving the whole vegetable, stuffed and baked. Small squashes can be baked whole, hollowed out and used as bowls for salads or soups.

Mushrooms

Lots of different mixed mushrooms are available in spring and summer, but they are most plentiful and varied during the autumn. Washing them makes them soggy, so just use kitchen towel or a soft brush to take off any specks of dirt.

Onions

Generally, the larger the onion, the milder the taste. Red onions are sweeter than brown onions and are the best choice for using raw in salads. Shallots have a delicate flavour – covering them with boiling water makes them easier to peel.

Jerusalem artichokes

Knobbly little roots with a sweet nutty flavour, these are relatives of the sunflower and no relation to globe artichokes, despite their name. Scrub them with a vegetable brush and steam them, then slice and serve warm with butter or an oil-based dressing.

Okra

Also called lady's fingers, okra is an unripe seed pod and should be eaten while it is young and green, as older specimens can be fibrous. It adds a thick, almost gluey consistency to stews, which some love and others hate!

Savoy cabbage

This cabbage has distinctive wrinkled leaves that are dark green on the outside and paler inside. Slice the leaves crossways into ribbons and stir-fry with onion and garlic, or blanch whole leaves and fold them around a savoury stuffing mixture.

Leeks

Soil and grit can become trapped inside leeks as they grow. To avoid a nasty crunch, cut off the root and any tough green leaves, then halve the leek lengthways, put into a sink full of cold water and separate the layers to clean them.

Chicory

Chicory heads should have greenish-white crisp leaves, firmly packed together. Sliced, they add a refreshing bitter taste to salads. Whole leaves can serve as tiny edible plates for canapés.

185 Sun-dried tomato and pumpkin seed pâté

(V)

Serves 4

Ingredients
- 140 g pumpkin seeds
- 8 sun-dried tomato halves in oil
- 1 clove garlic
- 2 tablespoons lemon juice
- 1 tablespoon soy sauce
- 1 large date
- ½ red chilli
- 2 spring onions

Preparation
The night before, soak the pumpkin seeds in cold water for six hours. Rinse and drain.

Whizz all of the ingredients except the spring onions in a food processor until semi-smooth. Decant the mixture into a small bowl. Finely chop the spring onions and mix into the bowl, reserving a few pieces to garnish.

Serve in individual ramekins with thickly sliced fresh bread or toast.

186 Thai-style mushrooms in chicory leaves

Makes about 30 canapés

Ingredients
- 140 g shiitake mushrooms
- 70 g radishes
- ½ small red pepper
- 6 heads of chicory

For the marinade
- 1 teaspoon chopped green chilli
- 1 cm ginger root
- ½ teaspoon garlic
- 2 tablespoons soy sauce
- 1 lime
- 1 tablespoon honey

Preparation
Start with the marinade. Finely chop the ginger root and zest and juice the lime, then mix with all the marinade ingredients in a bowl.

Chop the mushrooms, radishes and pepper and marinate. Stir thoroughly. Cover and refrigerate for one hour.

Cut off the bases of the chicory and take them apart. Set aside the hearts for use in a salad. Put a heaped teaspoon of the mushroom mixture into each of the larger leaves.

187 Leek and potato soup

Serves 4

Ingredients

- 1 tablespoon cumin seeds
- 450 g leeks
- 225 g potatoes
- 55 g salted butter
- 600 ml vegetable stock
- 275 ml milk
- 90 ml single cream
- Salt and freshly ground white pepper
- Chilli oil (optional)

Preparation

Dry-roast the cumin seeds in a heavy-bottomed saucepan for a minute or two, until they begin to release their aroma. Remove from the heat and set aside.

Peel and slice the leeks and potatoes. In a large saucepan, melt the butter and cook the leeks and potatoes, covered, for around 10 minutes, until soft but not coloured. Add the vegetable stock, bring to the boil and simmer, covered, for around 20 minutes, until the potatoes are tender.

Leave to cool slightly before blending in a blender or food processor. Stir in the milk and single cream, and adjust the seasoning to taste. Reheat to serve, topped with a few toasted cumin seeds and a drop of chilli oil.

188 Extra quick cornbread

Makes 9

Ingredients

- 70 g plain flour
- 70 g cornmeal
- 1 ½ teaspoons baking powder
- ½ teaspoon salt
- 1 medium egg
- 150 ml milk
- 1 tablespoon honey
- 1 tablespoon olive oil
- 1 green chilli (optional)

Preparation

Preheat the oven to 200°C. Grease a 18-cm round baking tin or a nine-hole muffin tin.

Sift the flour, cornmeal, baking powder and salt together in a large bowl. In a separate bowl, beat the egg and add the milk, honey and oil. Finely chop the green chilli, if using, and add to the bowl of dry ingredients. Mix thoroughly.

Combine the liquid ingredients with the dry ingredients and stir together to make a soft batter. Spoon into the prepared baking tin and bake for around 15 minutes, or until risen, golden brown and firm to the touch.

Serve warm, in buttered wedges with a bowl of soup or vegetable chilli.

189 Carrot and fennel soup

Serves 4

Ingredients

- 2 fennel bulbs
- 1 stick celery
- 1 onion
- 3 tablespoons olive oil
- 450 g carrots
- 2 cloves garlic
- 1 litre vegetable stock
- 2 tablespoons crème fraîche or sour cream, plus extra for serving
- Salt and freshly ground black pepper

Preparation

Thinly slice the fennel, celery and onion and fry in the olive oil until soft but not browned. Peel and chop the carrots and garlic and add to the pan. Cook for another minute or two. Pour in the vegetable stock, bring to the boil, cover and simmer for 20 minutes, until carrots are tender.

Remove from the heat and leave to cool slightly before stirring in the crème fraîche or sour cream. Blend the soup until smooth. Taste and adjust the seasoning, then reheat to serve. Top each bowl with a swirl of cream.

Fennel has a delicate aniseed flavour that works well with the sweetness of the carrots in this classic soup. Enjoy it hot or cold.

190 Sweet beetroot salad with orange and coconut

Serves 4

Ingredients
- 3 beetroots
- ½ orange
- 2 tablespoons fresh, grated coconut
- Juice ½ lime
- 2 tablespoons currants
- 1 teaspoon apple cider vinegar
- 1 teaspoon flaxseed oil

Preparation
Peel and finely grate the raw beetroots. Peel and dice the orange. Combine all the ingredients and chill for an hour before serving.

For an elegant presentation, pack small portions of the salad into ramekins, timbale moulds or espresso cups and turn out onto serving plates.

191 Blackberry and feta salad

Serves 4

Ingredients
- 125 g mixed salad greens
- 115 g feta cheese
- 300 g blackberries

For the vinaigrette
- 4 tablespoons olive oil
- 4 tablespoons balsamic vinegar
- 4 tablespoons honey

Preparation
Arrange the greens on plates and top with crumbled feta and blackberries, keeping about a dozen for the dressing.

To make the dressing, mash the remaining blackberries through a sieve and whisk the juice with the olive oil, balsamic vinegar and honey. Dress each plate individually.

Remember this recipe when you've found some ripe wild blackberries. The sweet-sharp fruit works perfectly with the salty cheese, and the colours are a treat. Feta also makes a great salad with watermelon (see page 96).

192 Jerusalem artichoke salad

Serves 4

Ingredients
- 450 g Jerusalem artichokes
- 1 large chicory
- 1 small red pepper

For the dressing
- 2 tablespoons lemon juice
- 2 tablespoons olive oil
- Salt and freshly ground black pepper
- 1 spring onion
- Handful fresh dill or thyme

Preparation
Scrub the Jerusalem artichokes but leave the skins on. Cut them into 0.5-cm slices and steam for 12 minutes, until soft but not breaking up. Shred the chicory. Slice the red pepper into thin matchsticks.

To make the dressing, blend the lemon juice, oil and seasoning. Finely chop the spring onion and herbs and stir in. Toss the vegetables in the dressing.

This salad is delicious warm or chilled.

193 Walnut and red grape salad

Serves 4

Ingredients
- 1 tablespoon salted butter
- 2 tablespoons caster sugar
- 55 g walnuts or pecans
- 2 heads chicory
- 115 g rocket leaves
- 55 g seedless red grapes
- 115 g blue cheese
- Salt and freshly ground black pepper

For the dressing
- 2 tablespoons olive oil
- 1 tablespoon balsamic vinegar

Preparation
Heat the butter and sugar in a small pan, add the nuts and cook gently, stirring continuously for five minutes until crisp. Turn onto a plate to cool slightly.

To make the dressing, blend the oil and vinegar and season to taste.

Cut the bases off the chicory, break into leaves and toss with the rocket and dressing. Top the salad with the red grapes, crumbled cheese and caramelised nuts.

194 Classic butternut squash soup

Serves 4

Ingredients

- 2 cloves garlic
- 2 tablespoons olive oil
- 3 sprigs fresh rosemary
- 1 butternut squash
- 2 carrots
- 1 onion
- 1 large potato
- 1 litre vegetable stock
- Stock, milk or single cream, to thin
- Salt and freshly ground black pepper

Preparation

Peel and crush the garlic. Heat the oil in a large saucepan and add the garlic and rosemary and warm for one minute. Peel and chop the squash, carrots and onion, and cube the potato. Add them to the pan and stir. Cook for 10 minutes, stirring regularly, then add the vegetable stock, turn down the heat and simmer, covered, for 30 minutes, until the vegetables are meltingly soft.

Allow the soup to cool, remove the rosemary sprigs and blend until smooth. If the soup is too thick, adjust by adding a little more stock, milk or single cream. Season to taste. Reheat to serve.

The garlic and rosemary in this soup provide a welcoming aroma that can't be beaten after a walk in the autumn woods. Garnish each bowl of soup with a swirl of sour cream, crème fraîche or herb pesto.

195 Vegan potato salad with apple and celery

Serves 4

Ingredients
- 4 large new potatoes
- 3 red-skinned apples
- 1 lemon
- 2 sticks of celery
- 55 g hazelnuts or pecans

For the vegan mayonnaise
- 90 ml chilled soya milk
- 1 clove garlic
- ½ teaspoon mustard
- 2 tablespoons lemon juice
- 160 ml vegetable oil

Preparation

Boil the potatoes leaving the skins on. Leave to cool and then slice. Core the apples and slice thinly, again leaving the skins on. Cut the lemon in half and squeeze one half over the apples to stop them discolouring. Trim and slice the celery sticks. Roughly crush the nuts with the side of a knife.

To make the mayonnaise, put the chilled soya milk, garlic and mustard into a blender with rest of the lemon juice. Blend briefly. Then, keeping the motor running, slowly drizzle in the oil and continue blending until the mixture thickens.

Toss all the salad ingredients together with 3 tablespoons of vegan mayonnaise and serve immediately.

196 Mushroom pâté with nutmeg and chives

Serves 4

Ingredients
- 2 shallots
- 55 g salted butter
- 225 g mixed mushrooms
- 25 g fresh breadcrumbs
- 100 g cottage cheese
- Pinch nutmeg
- Few fresh chives
- Salt and freshly ground black pepper

Preparation

Slice the shallots and fry in the butter until soft but not browned. Wipe and chop the mushrooms and add to the pan. Cover the pan and cook on a very low heat for 15 minutes. Leave to cool slightly.

Put the mushroom mixture into a food processor with the breadcrumbs, cottage cheese, nutmeg, chives and seasoning. Blend until smooth and transfer into a small bowl. Cover and refrigerate for an hour before serving.

Serve in individual ramekins with hot toast and a few crisp salad leaves.

197 Walnut and curly endive salad

Serves 4

Ingredients
- 225 g frisée (curly endive leaves)
- 225 g radicchio leaves
- 115 g walnuts

For the dressing
- Juice and zest ½ orange
- 2 tablespoons walnut oil
- 1 tablespoon olive oil
- 1 tablespoon balsamic vinegar
- 1 tablespoon soy sauce
- 1 teaspoon honey or maple syrup

Preparation
Trim the salad and chop or rip into bite-sized pieces. Chop the walnuts roughly and dry-roast in a heavy-bottomed saucepan for a few minutes.

To make the dressing, combine the orange juice and zest with the rest of the dressing ingredients. Pour over the salad and mix thoroughly to coat. Sprinkle the nuts on top and serve immediately.

198 Spinach and apricot salad

Serves 4

Ingredients
- 150 ml cider vinegar
- 2 tablespoons lemon juice
- 115 g dried apricots
- 140 g sunflower seeds
- 2 tablespoons soy sauce
- 2 tablespoons olive oil
- Freshly ground black pepper
- 700 g baby leaf spinach

Preparation
Heat the vinegar to boiling, then remove from heat. Add the lemon juice and put the dried apricots into the hot liquid to soak for 30 minutes.

Dry-roast the sunflower seeds in a heavy-bottomed saucepan until they begin to change colour. Take the pan off the heat, sprinkle on the soy sauce and mix thoroughly. Quickly scoop the sticky mixture out of the pan and onto a plate to cool.

Drain and chop the apricots, reserving the liquid. Whisk the reserved juice with the olive oil and black pepper to taste. Assemble the salad by mixing the spinach with the chopped apricots, sunflower seeds and dressing.

199 Creamy mushroom soup

Serves 4

Ingredients
- 2 onions
- 450 g mixed mushrooms
- 1 tablespoon olive oil
- 1 teaspoon paprika
- 1 teaspoon caraway seeds
- 500 ml water or vegetable stock
- 2 tablespoons margarine
- 3 tablespoons plain flour
- 275 ml non-dairy milk
- 2 to 3 tablespoons red wine
- Few sprigs fresh parsley

Preparation

Chop the onions and wipe and slice the mushrooms.
In a large saucepan, fry the onion in the olive oil until
soft and beginning to brown. Stir in the chopped
mushrooms, paprika and caraway seeds, and cook for
five minutes. Pour in the vegetable stock or water and
simmer, covered, for 15 minutes.

In a separate small saucepan, melt the margarine,
add the flour and cook for one minute, stirring
constantly. Add the non-dairy milk, a little at a time,
beating thoroughly to prevent lumps. Combine the
two mixtures, stir well, then simmer, covered, for 15
minutes. Finely chop the parsley. Stir the red wine into
the soup just before serving garnished with the parsley.

200 Squash salad with grapefruit and almonds

Serves 4

Ingredients

- 85 g brown rice
- ½ butternut squash
- 2 tablespoons vegetable oil
- Salt and freshly ground pepper
- 85 g whole, blanched almonds
- Cayenne pepper, to taste
- ½ tablespoon vegetable oil
- Few sprigs fresh mint
- Zest 1 lemon

For the dressing

- 1 grapefruit
- 1 shallot
- 1 tablespoon honey
- 2 tablespoons olive oil

Preparation

Preheat the oven to 180°C.

Cook the brown rice in a pan of boiling water for about 20 minutes, until soft. Drain and leave to cool. Peel, de-seed and cut the squash into 2.5-cm chunks. Toss in vegetable oil, season with salt and pepper and roast in a baking dish for around 30 minutes. Stir and return to the oven for a further 12 minutes, until soft and beginning to brown at the edges. Set aside to cool.

To toast the almonds, increase the oven temperature to 200°C. Put the blanched almonds into a small bowl and combine with the cayenne pepper and vegetable oil. Mix thoroughly and transfer to a baking tray. Toast for approximately five minutes, until fragrant and browning. The nuts become crisp as they cool. Chop the mint.

To make the citrus dressing, juice the grapefruit and dice the shallot. Combine both with the honey in a blender. Begin processing, and slowly add the olive oil. Adjust seasoning to taste.

To assemble the salad, mix the cooked, cooled butternut squash with the cooked rice and stir in the dressing. Sprinkle the lemon zest on top of the salad with the toasted almond and chopped mint. Serve immediately.

201 Warm broccoli salad

Serves 4

Ingredients
- 1 head broccoli
- 1 clove garlic
- 1 cm ginger root
- 1 teaspoon toasted sesame oil
- ½ teaspoon soy sauce
- ½ teaspoon chilli flakes
- 2 tablespoons cashew pieces

Preparation
Trim the broccoli and cut the florets into bite-sized pieces. Use a vegetable peeler to peel the stalk and chop it into crudité-sized sticks. Peel and crush the garlic. Peel and grate the ginger. Warm the sesame oil in a large saucepan or wok. Stir-fry the broccoli with the soy sauce, garlic, ginger, chilli and cashews for five minutes, until cooked but still crisp. Serve warm.

202 Warm roast beetroot and herb salad

Serves 4

Ingredients
- 700 g beetroot
- 2 cloves garlic
- Small handful fresh parsley
- Small handful fresh basil
- 4 tablespoons olive oil
- 1 tablespoon white wine vinegar
- 2 tablespoons capers

Preparation
Preheat the oven to 170°C.

Roast the whole beetroots for about an hour. Leave to cool for 15 minutes until cool enough to handle. Rub off the skin and slice into rounds. Peel and chop the garlic. Chop the parsley and basil. Mix the beetroots with all the other ingredients and serve warm.

203 Apple, walnut and goat's cheese salad

Serves 4

Ingredients

- 50 g walnut pieces
- 2 sticks celery
- 1 green-skinned apple
- 1 red-skinned apple
- 85 g mixed salad leaves

For the dressing

- 115 g soft rindless goat's cheese
- 2 tablespoons milk
- 1 teaspoon maple syrup
- 1 teaspoon white wine vinegar
- 2 tablespoons olive oil
- Salt and freshly ground black pepper

Preparation

Make the dressing first. Blend all the ingredients except the salt and pepper together in a food processor or blender. Having the goat's cheese at room temperature will help to bring it together smoothly. Taste, and adjust seasoning.

Toast the walnut pieces gently in a dry, heavy-bottomed saucepan for up to three minutes, until they begin to brown and release their fragrant oils, then turn onto a plate so that they do not cook any further.

Trim and chop the celery into bite-sized pieces. Core and thinly slice the apples, leaving the skins on.

Put the salad on a serving dish, top with the walnuts, apple and celery and drizzle with dressing, taking care not to swamp the fresh ingredients.

Celebrate the apple harvest by looking for some unusual or heritage varieties to try in this salad.

Five ways with potatoes

204
Rösti
Coarsely grate raw potatoes, mix with finely chopped onion and garlic, and gently fry spoonfuls of the mixture. Cook for five minutes on each side, flattening with the back of an oiled spoon.

205
Spicy wedges
Cut large baking potatoes into wedges; toss with olive oil, smoked paprika and cayenne pepper. Oven roast for 30 minutes at 200°C.

206
Twice baked
Scoop out the centre of baked potatoes and mix with chopped onion or finely grated leek, grated cheese and a splash of milk. Pile the stuffing back into the skins and bake in the oven for 15 minutes.

207
Potato salad
Toss boiled new potatoes in a flavourful vinaigrette or with mayonnaise and chopped spring onions. Mix it up by adding a little garlic or fresh chopped herbs, such as chives, sorrel or dill weed.

208
Sliced and baked
Slice potatoes very thinly using a mandolin or food processor. Layer in a baking dish with finely chopped rosemary, salt and black pepper. Pour over vegetable stock or cream to just cover the potatoes. Cover with foil and bake for an hour at 180°C. Remove the foil for the last 15 minutes of cooking.

209 Wild mushroom tartlets

Serves 4

Ingredients
- 15 g dried mushrooms
- 1 sheet ready-rolled puff pastry
- 400 g mixed wild mushrooms
- 2 tablespoons olive oil
- 2 tablespoons crème fraîche
- 2 egg yolks
- Salt and freshly ground black pepper

Preparation
Soak the dried mushrooms in boiling water for an hour. Drain and pat dry on kitchen towel, reserving the water. Using a 5-cm pastry cutter, cut 24 circles from the pastry sheet. Gently press each into a greased tartlet tin. Prick with a fork, then cover and chill.

Preheat the oven to 200°C. Roughly chop the mushrooms and fry in the olive oil for five minutes. Chop the drained, soaked mushrooms, add to the pan and cook for two minutes more. Leave to cool, then transfer to a food processor and blend to a rough paste, or chop very finely by hand. Transfer the chopped mushrooms to a large bowl, and beat in the crème fraîche, egg yolks and seasoning.

Fill each puff-pastry shell with a heaped teaspoon of mixture – they will rise and expand when cooked, so don't overfill. Bake for up to 12 minutes, until golden and springy to the touch. Serve warm with a drizzle of white truffle oil and a sprinkle of finely chopped herbs.

210 Wild mushroom salad

Serves 4

Ingredients
- 450 g mixed wild mushrooms
- 85 g mixed salad leaves
- 25 g salted butter
- Salt and freshly ground black pepper

For the dressing
- 2 tablespoons olive oil
- Zest ½ lemon
- 1 tablespoon balsamic vinegar

Preparation
Trim and wipe the mushrooms. This dish looks best if you keep the mushrooms whole – if there are any very large ones, halve or quarter them to match the size of the rest.

Arrange the salad on serving plates. Prepare the dressing by mixing the olive oil, lemon zest and balsamic vinegar together. Season to taste.

Melt the butter in a large heavy-bottomed pan and gently fry the mushrooms for three minutes, until heated through but not collapsing. Season with salt and pepper.

Arrange the warm mushrooms, along with any juices, on top of the salad and pour the dressing over the top. Serve warm with thickly sliced fresh bread.

211 Roasted onions stuffed with saffron rice

Serves 4

Ingredients

- 4 large onions
- 85 g basmati rice
- Pinch saffron strands
- 25 g salted butter
- 55 g pine nuts
- 2 tablespoons sultanas
- ½ teaspoon ground cardamom
- Salt and freshly ground black pepper
- Olive oil, for greasing
- 1 to 2 teaspoons caster sugar

Preparation

Preheat the oven to 200°C.

Put the whole onions, unpeeled, on a baking tray and roast for 45 minutes. When they are cool enough to handle, carefully trim the bases so that they will stand up, and trim a similar amount off the tops. Then peel the onions and press or scoop out the centres, retaining them for later and leaving the shells of the onions two to three layers thick.

Cook the rice with the saffron in boiling water for 10 minutes, until tender, then drain and set aside.

Finely chop the centres of the onions. Melt the butter in a large frying pan and gently cook the pine nuts for a minute, then stir in the chopped onion, sultanas and cardamom and fry until the onions are soft and translucent. Season to taste with salt and pepper.

Brush the onion shells with olive oil and sprinkle with a little caster sugar. Put them on a baking tray lined with baking parchment and carefully fill them with the stuffing. Return to the oven and bake for 20 minutes, until just browning.

212 Red wine mushroom bourguignon

Serves 4

Ingredients

- 3 large carrots
- 3 sticks celery
- 25 g button mushrooms
- 4 whole cloves garlic
- 450 g baby onions
- Few sprigs fresh thyme
- 4 tablespoons olive oil
- 750 ml vegetable stock
- 3 tablespoons tomato purée
- 1 tablespoon vegetarian Worcestershire sauce
- 450 ml red wine
- 1 tablespoon plain flour
- 2 bay leaves

Preparation

Trim and chop the carrots and celery. Wipe the mushrooms. Peel the garlic cloves. Peel the baby onions and cut any large ones in half. Strip the thyme leaves from their stalks and finely chop. Heat 2 tablespoons of the olive oil in a large flameproof casserole dish and fry the mushrooms for three minutes. Remove with a slotted spoon and set aside. Put the rest of the oil into the dish and fry the onions, garlic, carrots and celery until the onions are soft and translucent.

Put the stock into a large jug and mix in the tomato paste, Worcestershire sauce, thyme and wine.

Stir the flour into the vegetables and cook for a minute, then pour in the stock mixture and add the bay leaves. Cover and simmer for 20 minutes. Just before serving, stir in the mushrooms and heat through.

Most brands of Worcestershire sauce contain anchovies and are not suitable for vegetarians. Look for a vegetarian brand in a specialist food shop or in the 'healthy' section of the supermarket, or use mushroom ketchup. It's well worth having this versatile and tasty sauce in your store cupboard.

213 Wild mushroom sauté

Serves 4

Ingredients

- 4 shallots
- 900 g mixed wild mushrooms
- 125 ml olive oil
- 4 tablespoons salted butter
- 4 cloves garlic
- 3 tablespoons chopped
  flat-leaf parsley
- Freshly ground black pepper

Preparation

Blanch the shallots in a bowl of boiling water for a few minutes to loosen the skins. Peel and finely chop. Wipe the mushrooms, remove and discard any woody stems, then chop into roughly similar sizes – halves, quarters and slices. Gently cook the shallots in the oil for five minutes, until translucent, add the mushrooms and butter, then continue to cook over a medium heat for 10 minutes, stirring often so they don't stick.

Peel, chop and add the garlic and cook for a further two minutes. Remove from the heat, toss with chopped parsley and black pepper, and serve.

This works well as a side dish, or as a light meal served with crusty bread or brown rice.

214 Apricot and orange quinoa

Serves 4

Ingredients

- 10 dried apricots
- Juice and zest ½ orange
- 225 g quinoa
- Small handful fresh,
  flat-leaf parsley
- 2 tablespoons olive oil
- 50 g pine nuts
- ½ teaspoon cumin
- 55 g toasted flaked almonds

Preparation

Roughly chop the dried apricots and put them into a small bowl with the orange juice and 3 tablespoons of boiling water. Put the quinoa in a pan, cover with boiling water and simmer for 15 minutes. Turn off the heat and drain away any remaining water, then return the cooked quinoa to the warm pan, cover and allow to rest for five minutes before fluffing with a fork.

Chop the parsley. Drain the soaked apricots and gently mix them into the quinoa along with the orange zest, olive oil, parsley, pine nuts and cumin. Serve warm, sprinkled with flaked almonds.

215 Warm Japanese hijiki stir-fry

Serves 4

Ingredients

- 25 g dried hijiki seaweed
- 1 tablespoon plus 2 teaspoons soy sauce
- 2 carrots
- 115 g baby corn
- 2 spring onions
- 225 g mangetout
- ½ teaspoon dried red chilli flakes
- 1 tablespoon olive oil
- 1 teaspoon roasted sesame oil
- 1 tablespoon water
- 1 teaspoon cider vinegar or rice vinegar
- 1 tablespoon soy sauce
- 1 tablespoon cashew nuts

Preparation

Soak the hijiki in a pan of cold water for 30 minutes. Add 2 teaspoons of soy sauce to the soaking water, simmer for five minutes, then drain.

Cut the vegetables into pieces: matchstick-sized carrots, slices of baby corn and shredded spring onions and mangetout. Put them all into a large bowl with the chilli flakes, olive oil and roasted sesame oil, and mix thoroughly.

Stir-fry the vegetables in a hot, lightly oiled wok until heated through. Add the hijiki and splash in the water, vinegar and a tablespoon of soy sauce. Serve topped with a few whole cashews.

Hijiki is a sea vegetable that is popular in Japan. It is generally sold dried.

216 Warm kale with balsamic figs

Serves 4

Ingredients

- 200 g kale

For the dressing

- 5 dried figs
- 40 ml balsamic vinegar
- 115 ml olive oil
- ¼ teaspoon mild chilli powder
- 1 teaspoon lemon juice
- Salt and freshly ground black pepper

Preparation

Make the dressing first. Put the figs, balsamic vinegar, olive oil, chilli powder and lemon juice into a blender and process until smooth and creamy. Adjust seasoning to taste.

To cook the kale, strip out any tough stems, shred the leaves and boil for seven minutes. Drain, toss with the dressing and serve immediately.

217 Pumpkin and pear stew with saffron

Serves 4

Ingredients
- 2 cloves garlic
- 115 g bread
- 3 tablespoons olive oil
- 55 g ground almonds
- 1 teaspoon paprika
- 1 onion
- 125 ml dry white wine
- 115 g carrots
- 115 g pumpkin or squash
- 4 firm pears
- 1 x 400 g tin chopped tomatoes
- Few strands saffron
- 225 g cooked or tinned chickpeas

Preparation
Preheat the oven to 220°C.

Peel and crush the garlic. Slice the bread thickly and brush with 1 tablespoon of olive oil and crushed garlic. Put on a baking tray and bake until golden. Leave to cool, then break into pieces. Blend in a food processor with the almonds and paprika until smooth.

Chop the onion, and fry in the remaining olive oil in a large saucepan, until soft. Add the wine and 750 ml of water. Bring to the boil.

Peel and slice the carrots. Peel and cube the pumpkin. Core and cube the pear. Add to the saucepan along with the tomatoes and saffron and simmer for 15 minutes until the vegetables are tender. Stir in the bread paste and the chickpeas, and reheat to serve. This hearty stew makes a complete meal.

Some crusty bread is perfect for mopping up the stew!

218 Steamed lemon vegetable parcels

Serves 4

Ingredients
- 350 g prepared seasonal vegetables: baby carrots, winter squash, sprouting broccoli, green beans, spring onions, beansprouts, squash, baby corn, mushrooms, onions
- 2.5 cm ginger root
- 2 tablespoons olive oil
- Salt and freshly ground black pepper
- 1 lemon
- 4 tablespoons toasted flaked almonds

Preparation
Preheat the oven to 200°C.

Choose a mixture of colourful seasonal vegetables and cut them into fine slices. Peel and grate the ginger. Toss the vegetables with the olive oil, ginger and seasoning.

Thinly slice the lemon into rounds and divide between six large squares of baking parchment, then pile the prepared vegetables on top. Sprinkle with toasted flaked almonds and bring the corners of the parchment up to form pouches. Secure with natural fibre twine, place on a baking tray and bake for 15 minutes.

Serve the parcels on individual plates and let guests open them themselves (careful, the steam will hiss!).

219 Spinach and ricotta frittata

Makes 12

Ingredients
- 450 g spinach
- 250 g vegetarian ricotta cheese
- 2 tablespoons crème fraîche
- 55 g strong Cheddar cheese
- 4 medium eggs
- 60 ml milk
- ¼ teaspoon hot pepper sauce
- Pinch nutmeg
- Salt and freshly ground black pepper

Preparation
Preheat the oven to 190°C. Lightly grease a 12-cup muffin tin.

Blanch the spinach for two minutes, until it collapses. Lift out, drain and squeeze dry. Mix with the ricotta, crème fraîche and grated Cheddar cheese. Beat together the eggs, milk, hot pepper sauce, nutmeg, and salt and pepper. Stir into the spinach mixture.

Spoon the mixture into the prepared muffin tin and bake for around 25 minutes, until risen and golden. Allow to stand for five minutes before removing from the pan.

220 Butternut squash and Gruyère tart

Serves 4

Ingredients

- ½ large butternut squash
- 3 tablespoons olive oil
- Salt and freshly ground black pepper
- 55 g hazelnuts
- 1 large onion
- 2 cloves garlic
- 2 tablespoons dry white wine
- 115 g Gruyère cheese
- 1 medium egg
- ½ sheet ready-rolled puff pastry

Preparation

Preheat the oven to 200°C.

Peel and cube the squash and toss with 2 tablespoons of the olive oil, season with salt and pepper and roast on a greased baking tray for around 30 minutes, stirring occasionally, until beginning to brown.

Roast the hazelnuts on a baking tray for five minutes, leave to cool and crush coarsely.

Thinly slice the onion and chop the garlic and fry in a tablespoon of olive oil until brown. Stir in the wine and cook for a further minute. Grate the Gruyère and mix with the roasted squash, adding the onions and hazelnuts. Beat and mix in the egg.

Cut a 20 x 20-cm square from the pastry sheet and put onto a lightly greased baking tray and, using a sharp knife, score a line approximately 2 cm inside each edge. Pile the filling onto the pastry and arrange within the scored line – this allows the edges of the tart to puff up during baking. Bake for 15 minutes or until golden and serve immediately.

221 Courgette and rice bake

Serves 4

Ingredients

- 3 onions
- 2 cloves garlic
- 450 g courgettes
- 115 g Cheddar cheese
- 2 tablespoons olive oil
- 250 ml vegetable stock
- 100 g Arborio or other short-grain rice
- 2 medium eggs
- 200 ml crème fraîche
- ½ teaspoon smoked paprika

Preparation

Preheat the oven to 220°C.

Peel and finely slice the onions. Peel and crush the garlic. Thinly slice the courgettes. Grate the cheese. Fry the onions and courgettes in the oil for five minutes, until they begin to soften. Stir in the garlic and cook for a further minute, then add the vegetable stock and rice. Bring to the boil and reduce the heat to a minimum. Cover and cook very gently for 20 minutes.

Beat the eggs with the crème fraîche, paprika and half the cheese. Stir this into the rice, mix well and transfer to a greased baking dish. Top with the remaining cheese and a little more paprika, and bake for 15 minutes, until the cheese is golden and bubbling.

Use up the last of the season's courgettes in this satisfying cheesy dish, spiked with delicious smoked paprika.

222 Leeks à la grecque

Serves 4

Ingredients
- Juice 2 lemons
- 4 tablespoons olive oil
- 125 ml dry white wine
- 600 ml water
- 5 celery leaves
- 1 carrot
- 1 small onion
- 10 black peppercorns
- 10 whole coriander seeds
- 1 bay leaf
- 8 leeks
- 1 medium egg
- Handful black olives

Preparation
Mix the lemon juice with the oil, wine and water and place in a large saucepan. Peel and chop the celery leaves, carrot and onion. Add to the saucepan long with the peppercorns, coriander seeds and bay leaf. Bring to the boil, then simmer, covered, for 10 minutes.

Trim the leeks and cook them in the liquid until tender, about 10 minutes. Hard-boil the egg in the same water, approximately seven minutes. Allow the cooked leeks to cool in the liquid, then remove to a plate. Remove the boiled egg. Reduce the cooking liquid by boiling it fast. Leave to cool. Chop the egg.

To serve, strain the reduced liquid and pour over the leeks. Garnish with the chopped egg and black olives.

223 Broccoli with lemon butter

Serves 4

Ingredients
- 1 head broccoli
- 25 g flaked almonds
- 115 g salted butter
- Juice and zest ½ lemon

Preparation
Trim the broccoli and cut the florets into bite-sized pieces. Use a potato peeler to peel the stalk and slice it thinly into rounds. Steam the broccoli until bright green and tender, about five minutes. Put the flaked almonds into a small, heavy-bottomed pan and warm them gently until they begin to brown. Remove from the heat and transfer to a plate to prevent burning.

Melt the butter in a small saucepan, then stir in the lemon juice and zest with the toasted almonds. Pour over the warm broccoli and serve immediately.

Five ways with pumpkin or butternut squash

224
Honey-roasted chunks
Toss peeled chunks in a mixture of olive oil and honey and roast at 200°C until tender (about 30 minutes). Stir into a warm salad with some cooked grains, wilted spinach and soft goat's cheese.

225
Deep-fried tempura
Peel squash, cut into strips, coat in a beer batter (see page 94) and deep-fry. Serve at once with a dip of soy sauce, white wine vinegar, honey, sesame oil and finely chopped spring onions.

226
Fruity kebabs
Skewer peeled chunks of squash or pumpkin, baste with a marinade of pineapple juice, soy sauce, root ginger, garlic, olive oil and dry sherry, then grill or barbecue for 10 minutes, turning and basting frequently.

227
Crunchy wedges
Leave the skin on, and cut into 1-cm slices. Add oil, thyme, lemon zest and crushed garlic and bake at 190°C for 30 minutes.

228
Roasted seeds
Don't waste the seeds! Toss dried seeds with olive oil and season with garlic salt, ground cumin and coriander or try brown sugar, ground cinnamon and ginger. Roast at 150°C for 30 minutes. Serve as a snack, or sprinkled onto salad, fruit salad or porridge.

229 Tofu in hot sauce

Serves 4

Ingredients
- 1 pack (approx. 250 g) firm tofu
- 1 clove garlic
- 1 tablespoon toasted sesame oil
- 1 teaspoon soy sauce
- 1 teaspoon tomato purée
- 1 teaspoon hot paprika
- 1 tablespoon cornflour
- Fresh coriander

Preparation
Drain the tofu and cut into bite-sized pieces. Peel and crush the garlic. Warm the oil in a small saucepan or wok, and gently fry the garlic for just a moment or two, then remove from the heat.

Put the soy sauce, tomato paste and paprika into a small saucepan with 225 ml of cold water. Whisk together well, then beat in the cornflour. Heat the mixture gradually, stirring constantly, until boiling point is reached. Tip the garlic and oil into the sauce.

Gently stir the tofu into the sauce and heat through to serve. Garnish with sprigs of fresh coriander.

230 Leek and red lentil bake

Serves 4

Ingredients
- 200 g red lentils
- 450 g leeks
- 1 clove garlic
- 3 medium eggs
- 125 g strong Cheddar cheese
- 2 tablespoons olive oil
- Sprig fresh rosemary
- 100 g tinned chopped tomatoes
- Salt and freshly ground black pepper

Preparation

Preheat the oven to 200°C.

In a large saucepan, cover the lentils with water, bring to the boil and then simmer until completely soft, about 20 minutes. Add more water during cooking as necessary.

Trim and slice the leeks. Crush the garlic, beat the eggs and grate the Cheddar cheese. Fry the leeks in the olive oil until soft, about five minutes. Add the garlic and rosemary and cook for a minute or two.

Combine the lentils, leeks and all the remaining ingredients. Mix thoroughly and pile into a greased baking dish. Bake for 30 minutes until set and golden.

231 Pan-fried baby carrot barlotto

Serves 4

Ingredients
- 600 ml vegetable stock
- 225 g barley
- 1 tablespoon soy sauce
- 3 tablespoons salted butter
- 2 cloves garlic
- 12 whole baby carrots
- 2 tablespoons vegetable oil
- 4 sprigs fresh thyme
- Salt and freshly ground black pepper

Preparation

In a large saucepan, bring the stock to the boil, using just enough to cover the barley. Add a dash of soy sauce and the barley and simmer for 45 minutes. Stir in a tablespoon of butter.

Peel the garlic and halve lengthways. Fry the carrots in the oil over a high heat for five minutes, turning frequently. Add the thyme, garlic and the remaining butter. Stir to coat the carrots, then add 125 ml of stock. Season and simmer, covered, for 20 minutes, until the carrots are tender.

Serve the barley topped with the carrots and their cooking liquid.

A barlotto is a risotto made with barley rather than Arborio rice.

232 Nutty onion tart

Serves 4

Ingredients

- 55 g Cheddar cheese
- 55 g unblanched almonds
- 85 g fresh wholemeal breadcrumbs
- Pinch nutmeg
- 2 teaspoons sunflower oil

For the filling

- 1 large onion
- 125 ml vegetable stock
- 1 teaspoon wholemeal flour
- Few fresh chives
- 1 medium egg
- 1 teaspoon Dijon mustard
- 150 ml plain yogurt
- Salt and freshly ground black pepper

Preparation

Preheat the oven to 200°C.

Grate the Cheddar cheese and put into the bowl of a food processor with the almonds and breadcrumbs. Process until you have fine crumbs. Stir in the nutmeg and sunflower oil, and press the mixture into a greased 18-cm pie tin to cover the bottom and sides. Bake for 10 minutes.

Peel and finely chop the onion. Simmer in 75 ml of the vegetable stock, uncovered, until the liquid has evaporated and the onion is soft. Reduce the heat and continue to cook for another minute or two, until the onion begins to colour. Stir in the flour, then stir in the remaining stock and remove from the heat. Leave to cool slightly. Chop the chives. Beat the egg and add to the cooled stock with the mustard, yogurt, chives and seasoning. Mix well. Spoon into the pie tin and return to the oven to bake for 15 minutes. Serve warm with a crisp green salad.

233 Golden baked okra

Serves 4

Ingredients

- 450 g okra
- 2 red peppers
- 1 onion
- 2 tablespoons vegetable oil
- 4 medium eggs
- 2 teaspoons dried mixed herbs
- 140 g Cheddar cheese

Preparation

Preheat the oven to 170°C.

Trim the okra and de-seed and chop the peppers. Peel and chop the onion. Gently fry the okra, onion and peppers in the oil for up to eight minutes, until all the vegetables are soft.

Beat the eggs with the dried herbs. Grate the Cheddar cheese and add to the eggs, mixing well. Combine the egg mixture with the cooked vegetables and spoon into a greased baking dish. Bake for 20 minutes, until cooked through, and puffy and golden.

This country-style recipe can be assembled in advance and slipped into the oven when you get home.

234 Autumn root vegetables glazed in cider

Serves 4

Ingredients

- 900 g prepared weight of mixed root vegetables: carrots, parsnips, turnips, sweet potatoes, celeriac, beetroot
- 2.5 cm preserved stem ginger
- 3 tablespoons salted butter
- 160 ml apple cider
- 3 tablespoons honey or maple syrup
- Salt and freshly ground black pepper
- Small handful fresh parsley

Preparation

Preheat the oven to 200°C.

Peel the root vegetables and chop into matchsticks. Finely chop the ginger.

Put the butter, cider, honey and ginger in a large, shallow baking dish and put into the oven to melt the butter. Remove, and stir to combine the ingredients. Add the prepared root vegetables to the dish, season and stir well to coat with the cider mixture. Cover with kitchen foil and bake for 30 minutes, then remove the foil, stir the vegetables and return to the oven. Bake for 20 minutes longer, or until the vegetables are tender. Chop the parsley and sprinkle over before serving.

This moist and colourful side dish works well with nutty casseroles or veggie burgers and baked potatoes.

235 Easy autumn risotto

Serves 4

Ingredients

- 1 clove garlic
- 1 small onion
- 225 g butternut squash
- 25 g salted butter or vegan margarine
- 115 g Arborio or other short-grain rice
- 1 tablespoon mixed herbs
- 300 ml vegetable stock
- 200 ml white wine
- Salt and freshly ground black pepper

Preparation

Preheat the oven to 180°C. Crush the garlic. Chop the onion. Peel and cube the butternut squash.

Put the butter and crushed garlic into a baking dish and put in the oven for two minutes, to melt. Add the chopped vegetables and return to the oven for five minutes. Stir in the rice, herbs, stock and wine and return to the oven for 40 minutes, stirring occasionally. Season to taste.

236 Leek, mint and feta terrine

Serves 4

Ingredients

- 1 kg young leeks, no more than 2.5-cm thick
- Handful fresh mint
- 140 g feta cheese
- Salt and freshly ground black pepper

Preparation

Line a 450-g loaf tin with several layers of cling film, letting it drape over the sides. Trim the leeks so that they fit neatly along the length of the pan, rinse thoroughly and then boil them in salted water for about 10 minutes, until soft. Drain, and arrange some of the leeks in one layer in the base of the prepared tin.

Chop the mint and crumble the feta. Sprinkle over the top of the leeks and season with salt and pepper. Continue building up the layers, ending with a layer of leeks, pressing down firmly so that the pan is well packed.

Wrap the flaps of cling film over the top of the terrine and weigh it down with another loaf tin filled with some kitchen weights or food tins. Refrigerate for three hours or overnight. To serve, carefully unwrap the terrine onto a chopping board. Slice slowly and carefully using a sharp, serrated knife and a gentle sawing motion.

Serve cold with a simple vinaigrette or a light mustard sauce.

237 Lemon millet with adzuki beans and corn

Serves 4

Ingredients

- 225 g millet
- ½ red onion
- Small handful fresh parsley
- 115 g tinned adzuki beans
- 115 g sweetcorn kernels

For the dressing

- Juice and zest ½ lemon
- 2 tablespoons olive oil
- ½ teaspoon ground coriander
- Freshly ground black pepper

Preparation

Toast the millet in a dry pan for three minutes. Add 500 ml of water, bring to the boil and then simmer, covered, for around 25 minutes or until all the water has been absorbed and the millet is tender. Set aside to cool.

Make the dressing. Juice and zest the lemon and mix together with the remaining dressing ingredients. Finely chop the red onion and the parsley. Fluff up the cooled millet and stir in the adzuki beans, finely chopped onion, sweetcorn, parsley and dressing. Serve chilled.

238 Aubergine and mozzarella bake

Serves 6

Ingredients

- 4 aubergines
- 225 g mozzarella cheese
- 100 g mature Cheddar cheese
- 6 tablespoons olive oil

For the sauce

- 2 onions
- 4 cloves garlic
- 2 tablespoons olive oil
- 4 x 400 g tins chopped tomatoes
- 1 bay leaf
- 1 teaspoon brown sugar
- Salt and freshly ground black pepper

Preparation

Preheat the oven to 180°C.

Make the tomato sauce first. Peel and finely chop the onions. Peel and chop the garlic. Fry the onions and garlic in the olive oil until translucent, add the tomatoes and bay leaf and simmer, stirring frequently, for 25 minutes, until thickened. Add the sugar and season to taste. Remove and discard the bay leaf.

Slice the aubergines lengthways into slices around 0.5-cm thick. Tear the mozzarella into pieces and grate the Cheddar cheese. Fry the aubergine in small batches, using the olive oil as required, until slightly coloured and soft. Layer the slices with the tomato sauce and cheeses in a 23 x 20-cm baking dish, beginning with aubergine and ending with a layer of cheese. Bake for up to 40 minutes, until golden and bubbling.

239 Savoury apple fritters

Makes 8

Ingredients

- 85 g plain flour
- 2 medium eggs
- 1 tablespoon milk
- 2 large cooking apples
- 115 g Cheddar cheese
- 250 g mozzarella cheese
- Few sprigs fresh thyme
- Salt and freshly ground black pepper
- 4 tablespoons vegetable oil, to fry

Preparation

Mix the flour, eggs and milk to make a thick batter. Grate the apples and Cheddar cheese, and cut up the mozzarella. Strip the thyme leaves from their stalks and chop. Stir into the batter, along with all the remaining ingredients except the oil. Mix thoroughly, and shape into small patties using extra flour to coat.

Shallow fry in small batches until crisp and golden, about one minute each side. Serve hot with the Red Onion Marmalade with Cinnamon (see right).

240 Red onion marmalade with cinnamon

Serves 4

Ingredients

- 55 g salted butter
- 200 g red onions
- 1 large cooking apple
- 50 ml red wine vinegar
- 1 tablespoon brown sugar
- 1 teaspoon ground cinnamon

Preparation

Melt the butter in a pan. Peel and slice the onions and gently fry until meltingly soft.

Peel, core and finely chop the apple. Add to the pan with the vinegar, sugar and cinnamon and simmer, uncovered, for 25 minutes. Serve warm or cold.

Try serving this chutney with the Carrot and Chilli Pancakes on the opposite page.

241 Carrot and chilli pancakes

Makes 12

Ingredients

- 2 medium eggs
- 115 g plain flour
- 150 ml milk
- 140 g carrots
- 1 green chilli
- 1 teaspoon cumin seeds
- 3 spring onions
- Salt and freshly ground black pepper

Preparation

Mix the eggs, flour and milk to make a smooth batter. Finely grate the carrots, de-seed and chop the chilli and stir in with the remaining ingredients.

Lightly grease a large heavy-bottomed frying pan and spoon a tablespoon or two of the batter onto the hot surface to make a few pancakes at a time. When the pancakes are dry on top, carefully turn and cook for another minute or two before transferring to a warm plate. Serve warm, with a spicy salsa, warm apple or cranberry sauce, or Red Onion Marmalade (see opposite).

242 Sweet-and-sour tofu

Serves 4

Ingredients

- 1 pack (approx. 250 g) firm tofu
- 2 tablespoons vegetable oil
- 4 tablespoons rice vinegar
- 175 ml pineapple juice
- 3 tablespoons brown sugar
- 1 tablespoon cornflour
- 2.5 cm ginger root
- 100 g pineapple chunks or pieces

Preparation

Drain the tofu and cut into slices or triangles. Gently fry in the oil, turning carefully until golden on both sides. Turn onto kitchen towel to drain.

In a saucepan away from the heat, beat the vinegar, pineapple juice, sugar and cornflour together with 4 tablespoons of cold water. Grate the ginger, then gather up all the gratings and squeeze out the juice. Add the ginger juice to the pan, discarding the pulp. Heat the mixture gently until boiling point is reached, beating constantly. Stir in the pineapple pieces and tofu and heat through, stirring gently, before serving.

243 Baked acorn squash

Serves 4

Ingredients

- 1 acorn squash
- Olive oil, for brushing
- 4 leeks
- 175 g cherry tomatoes
- 2 medium eggs
- 200 g Cheddar cheese
- Salt and freshly ground black pepper
- Small handful fresh basil

Preparation

Preheat the oven to 220°C.

Cut the squash in half from top to bottom. Scoop out and discard the seeds. Place cut-side down on a baking sheet lined with baking parchment and bake for 10 minutes. Cut out and reserve the flesh, leaving a shell about 1.5-cm thick. Brush the inside of the squash with a little olive oil, return to the baking sheet and bake for a further five minutes.

Trim and slice the leeks thinly, cut the tomatoes into halves and chop the reserved squash flesh into bite-sized pieces before adding to a large bowl. Beat the eggs, grate the cheese and mix with the vegetables. Season generously.

Pile the stuffing mixture into the squash shells, cover with kitchen foil and return to the oven for 30 minutes. Remove the foil and cook for a further 15 minutes or so, until browned and bubbling. Tear the fresh basil and sprinkle over the top of the squash before serving.

244 Spaghetti baked in parchment

Serves 6

Ingredients
- 450 g dried spaghetti
- 4 cloves garlic
- Small handful fresh, flat-leaf parsley
- 4 tablespoons olive oil
- 2 teaspoons dried red pepper flakes
- Sea salt flakes and freshly ground black pepper
- 6 tablespoons dry white wine

Preparation
Preheat the oven to 190°C.

Cook the spaghetti in salted, boiling water until just tender, drain and rinse with cold water.

Peel and crush the garlic and chop the parsley. Warm the oil in a small pan and fry the garlic and chilli flakes together for a minute or two. Remove from the heat and stir in the parsley, salt and pepper. In a large bowl, mix together the cooked spaghetti, garlic oil and white wine. Toss until well combined.

Divide the spaghetti between six large squares of baking parchment and fold the parchment around the pasta to form parcels. Put on a baking tray and bake for 15 minutes. Put each parcel on a serving plate and let guests open with care.

An unusual way to present a very simple dish! Serve with small bowls of pitted black olives, grated cheese, chopped sun-dried tomatoes, toasted pine nuts and capers, for guests to help themselves.

245 Mushroom and sage sausages

Serves 4

Ingredients

- 1 large onion
- 1 tablespoon vegetable oil
- 200 g wholemeal bread
- Handful fresh sage leaves
- 225 g button mushrooms
- 1 medium egg
- 150 g ground almonds
- Salt and freshly ground black pepper

Preparation

Finely chop the onion and fry in the oil until transparent. Put the bread and sage in a food processor and pulse to fine crumbs. Wipe and finely chop the mushrooms. Add to the breadcrumbs and pulse until well combined.

Beat the egg. Transfer the mushroom mixture to a large mixing bowl and stir in the cooked onion, ground almonds, beaten egg and seasoning. Shape the mixture into six or eight thick sausages and chill for at least 30 minutes.

Fry the sausages gently in a little vegetable oil, or brush them with oil, place on a baking tray lined with baking parchment and bake at 200°C for 25 minutes, until brown.

These sausages are good served in warmed bread rolls with corn relish or mustard and ketchup.

246 Leek and Cheddar sausages

Serves 4

Ingredients

- 2 leeks
- 140 g strong Cheddar cheese
- 3 tablespoons vegetable oil
- 300 g fresh white breadcrumbs
- 1 tablespoon wholegrain mustard
- 3 medium eggs
- Salt and freshly ground black pepper

Preparation

Wash and chop the leeks and grate the cheese. Cook the leeks in 1 tablespoon of the vegetable oil until softened. Transfer to a large bowl, and mix in 200 g of the breadcrumbs, the grated Cheddar, mustard and 2 of the eggs. Season and chill for 30 minutes.

Beat the remaining egg and place it in a shallow dish. Put the remaining breadcrumbs on a large plate next to it and season with salt and freshly ground black pepper. Shape the sausage mixture into eight sausages, dip into the beaten egg, then roll in the breadcrumbs until well coated. Gently fry the sausages in the oil for 10 minutes, until golden.

247 Hearty vegetarian sausage and cider casserole

Serves 4

Ingredients

- 450 g potatoes
- 1 large onion
- Few sprigs fresh thyme
- 3 tablespoons vegetable oil
- 1 large cooking apple
- 1 large carrot
- 1 x 400 g tin chopped tomatoes
- 1 tablespoon tomato purée
- 600 ml vegetable stock
- 6 vegetarian sausages
- 90 ml apple cider

Preparation

Peel the potatoes and parboil in a medium-sized saucepan. Cut into small chunks, then parboil again for two minutes. Drain. Chop the onion. Strip the thyme leaves from the stalks and chop. Fry the onion in the oil until beginning to brown, then stir in the thyme. Peel, core and cube the apple, peel and dice the carrot and add both to the pan.

Transfer to a large saucepan and add the tomatoes, tomato paste, stock and potatoes. Bring to the boil, then simmer until the potatoes and carrots are cooked through, about 10 minutes. Cook the vegetarian sausages and cut into chunks. Stir the apple cider into the pan and cook for another three minutes, then stir in the vegetarian sausage pieces and warm through before serving.

248 Sweet potato and okra casserole

Serves 4

Ingredients

- 700 g sweet potatoes
- 175 g okra
- 1 onion
- 1 red chilli
- 2.5 cm ginger root
- 1 tablespoon vegetable oil
- 600 ml vegetable stock
- 2 teaspoons cinnamon
- 1 x 400 g tin chopped tomatoes
- Small handful fresh coriander

Preparation

Peel the sweet potatoes and cut them into bite-sized pieces. Trim the okra and cut into slices. Peel and roughly chop the onion. De-seed and finely chop the chilli. Grate the ginger.

Warm the vegetable oil in a flameproof casserole dish and fry the onions gently until they are soft and translucent. Stir in the chilli, ginger and cinnamon and cook for a further minute. Stir in the sweet potatoes and stock, and simmer for five minutes, until the potatoes begin to soften. Add the chopped tomatoes and okra, stir together well, cover and simmer for a further 15 minutes or so, until all the vegetables are tender. Chop the coriander and sprinkle over the casserole before serving.

249 Green tomato chutney with cumin

Serves 4

Ingredients
- 1.3 kg small green tomatoes
- 700 ml white wine vinegar
- 900 g sugar
- ½ teaspoon ground cumin

Preparation
Drop the whole tomatoes in a large saucepan or bowl of boiling water, prick each one with the tip of a sharp knife and leave for one minute. Drain and transfer to a bowl of ice-cold water. The skins should split and the tomatoes will then be easy to peel. Put the peeled tomatoes into a large saucepan with the vinegar, sugar and cumin, and boil rapidly for five minutes.

To preserve the chutney, transfer it while still hot to sterilised jars and seal immediately. The seal will tighten as the chutney cools. Alternatively, the chutney can be stored in a jar or covered bowl in the refrigerator for a week.

Don't let those unripened tomatoes go to waste! This simple preserve works well with cheese and in sandwiches made with nut or bean pâtés. This is a perfect way to use up the last of the tomato crop – it works well with red or yellow tomatoes, too, and makes sure that nothing goes to waste.

250 Blackberry jelly

Serves 4

Ingredients

- 1.3 kg blackberries
- 2 large cooking apples
- 450 ml water
- Juice 1 lemon
- White sugar (see below for amount)

Preparation

Wash the blackberries for cobwebs and insects. Wash the apples, then skin, core and chop them. Bring the water to the boil in a large saucepan, add the blackberries, apple pieces and lemon juice and simmer for 20 minutes, until the fruit is soft.

Transfer the fruit and juice to a sterilised jelly bag suspended over a large bowl and leave it to drip overnight. A colander lined with washed muslin can also be used. Be patient and don't be tempted to squeeze the bag, because this will make the jelly cloudy.

Measure the juice in a jug and then return it to a preserving pan or very large saucepan. For every 600 ml of juice add 450 g of sugar. Bring to the boil and simmer for up to 15 minutes, spooning away any bubbly residue that forms.

To test for setting, chill a small plate. Put a spoonful of the hot jelly mixture onto the plate and place in the refrigerator for five minutes. Now push the edge of the jelly with your finger – if it wrinkles, setting point has been reached.

Carefully pour the hot liquid into sterilised jars, seal and store in a cool, dark place.

This jelly is not just for breakfast or sweet dishes; it is delicious with cheese and crackers too!

251 Mulled apple juice

Serves 4

Ingredients
- 1 large orange
- 1 litre apple juice
- 2 cinnamon sticks
- 5 cloves
- Honey, to taste

Preparation
Using a vegetable peeler or sharp knife, remove the zest of the orange in thick strips. Juice the orange.

Gently warm the apple juice, orange juice and zest, cinnamon and cloves in a pan for 10 minutes. Sweeten with honey to taste.

252 Pear and ginger zinger

Serves 4

Ingredients
- 3 firm pears
- 2.5 cm ginger root
- Juice ½ lemon
- Sparkling mineral water, to taste

Preparation
Juice the pears and the ginger. Add the lemon juice and dilute to taste with sparkling mineral water.

Best consumed immediately after making, this is a wonderfully refreshing breakfast juice.

253 Honey banana smoothie

Serves 4

Ingredients
- 1 ripe banana
- 350 ml milk or non-dairy alternative
- 1 to 2 tablespoons honey or maple syrup
- ¼ teaspoon ground nutmeg
- 3 ice cubes

Preparation
Put all the ingredients in a blender and blend until smooth. Serve immediately as a satisfying breakfast. Alternatively, omit the ice cubes and add a little more milk to the blended mixture. Transfer to a saucepan, warm gently and serve in heatproof glasses topped with a sprinkle of freshly ground nutmeg.

254 Almond chocolate milk

Serves 4

Ingredients
- 300 g almonds
- 1.5 litres cold water
- 3 dried dates
- 2 teaspoons carob or cocoa powder

Preparation
Working in batches, put the nuts and water in a blender and blend on high speed for several minutes. Combine and strain the mixture through two layers of muslin. Return the 'milk' to the blender and blend in the dates and carob or cocoa powder.

A healthy vegan alternative to a chocolate milkshake, sweetened with dates, this is always a hit with children!

255 Poached pears with hot chocolate sauce

Serves 4

Ingredients

- 1 vanilla pod
- 300 ml white or sweet wine
- 25 g caster sugar
- 2 tablespoons clear honey
- 1 cinnamon stick
- 4 pears
- 450 g plain chocolate
- 85 g unsalted butter

Preparation

Split the vanilla pod. Put the white wine, sugar, honey, cinnamon stick and split vanilla pod in a deep saucepan and heat to a gentle simmer. Carefully immerse the pears in the liquid. Poach over a low heat for 30 minutes, or until translucent, turning occasionally. Remove the pears from the pan, turn up the heat and continue to cook the liquid to make a pourable syrup.

Break up the chocolate and melt with the butter in a heatproof bowl over a saucepan of simmering water. When the mixture is smooth remove from the heat, but leave the bowl on the warm pan so that the sauce does not cool and set. Serve each pear on a pool of warm syrup, topped with the warm chocolate sauce.

A little vanilla ice cream is a lovely addition to this dish.

256 Apple and fig mille-feuille

Serves 6

Ingredients

- 1 lemon
- 5 medium cooking apples
- 225 g dried figs
- 250 ml apple cider
- 4 tablespoons sugar
- 1 teaspoon cinnamon
- 1 pack filo pastry
- 3 teaspoons icing sugar
- Vegetable oil, for brushing

Made with layers of crispy filo pastry, this is a classic pâtisserie. Mille-feuille means 'thousand leaves' in French.

Preparation

Preheat the oven to 400°F.

Using a vegetable peeler, peel the zest from the lemon in wide strips. Squeeze half the lemon. Peel and core the apples and cut into large chunks. Chop the figs.

In a 3-quart pan, mix together the lemon peel and juice, apple chunks, cider, chopped figs, sugar, and cinnamon. Cover and heat to boiling point, then reduce the heat and simmer, covered, for around 10 minutes, until the apples are just tender. Remove from the heat and let cool.

Separate one sheet of the phyllo pastry and lay it on a floured board. Brush it lightly with vegetable oil, and lay another sheet on top. Repeat to make a stack of four sheets of pastry. Using a sharp knife, carefully cut the stack of pastry sheets lengthwise into three equal strips. Then cut each strip into six equal rectangles.

Transfer the pastry stacks to a baking sheet lined with parchment paper and bake for up to eight minutes, until crisp and golden. Remove from the oven and transfer the cooked pastry pieces to a cooling rack.

Assemble the mille-feuille immediately before serving. Place one pastry piece on a serving plate and top with the apple and fig mixture. Put a second pastry piece on top of that and add more of the fruit. Finish with a final pastry piece and sprinkle with confectioners' sugar and a little more cinnamon to serve. Repeat with the remaining fruit mixture and pastry pieces until you have six mille-feuille towers.

257 Banana chocolate muffins

Makes 12

Ingredients

- 85 g unsalted butter
- 1 tablespoon honey
- 2 ripe bananas
- 250 g plain flour
- 1 teaspoon baking powder
- ½ teaspoon bicarbonate of soda
- Pinch salt
- Pinch nutmeg
- 115 g brown sugar
- 85 g dark chocolate
- 2 medium eggs
- 125 ml milk

Preparation

Preheat the oven to 190°C. Grease a muffin tin or line with paper or silicone cases.

Melt the butter, stir in the honey and set to one side to cool slightly. Mash the bananas. Sift the flour, baking powder, bicarbonate of soda, salt and nutmeg into a large mixing bowl. Add the sugar and chocolate in chunks, and mix well.

Beat the eggs with the milk, and add the cooled melted butter and honey. Stir in the mashed bananas. Stir the dry and wet mixtures together until just combined.

Divide the batter between the muffin cups and bake for 20 minutes, or until well risen and cooked through. Leave to cool for five minutes in the tin before transferring to a cooling rack.

258 Crunchy pear and cinnamon muffins

Makes 12

Ingredients

- 200 g plain flour
- 2 teaspoons baking powder
- 150 g soft brown sugar
- ½ teaspoon salt
- 3 teaspoons cinnamon
- 1 medium egg
- 4 tablespoons vegetable oil
- 4 tablespoons milk
- 2 pears
- 1 tablespoon pecans or walnuts
- 2 tablespoons demerara sugar

Preparation

Preheat the oven to 200°C. Grease a muffin tin or line with paper or silicone cases.

Sift the flour and baking powder together into a large mixing bowl, and stir in the sugar, salt and 2 teaspoons of the cinnamon. Beat the egg with the oil and milk. Pour into the flour and mix until just combined. Peel and chop the pears and fold in. Spoon the batter into the prepared muffin cups.

Chop or crush the nuts and mix into the demerara sugar and remaining cinnamon. Sprinkle over the muffins. Bake for 20 minutes, or until well risen and cooked through.

259 Black cherry and chocolate puffs

Makes 18

Ingredients

- 1 pack ready-rolled puff pastry
- 500 ml whipping cream
- 5 drops vanilla essence
- 4 tablespoons icing sugar
- Juice 1 lemon
- 85 g dark chocolate
- 3 tablespoons boiling water
- 30 stoned black cherries, fresh or tinned

Preparation

Preheat the oven to 180°C.

Using a sharp knife, cut the pastry lengthways into three equal strips. Then cut each strip into six equal pieces. Transfer the pastry pieces to a baking tray lined with baking parchment and bake for 15 minutes, or until puffy and golden. Transfer to a wire rack to cool.

Whip the cream together with the vanilla essence until fluffy. Mix the icing sugar with enough lemon juice and warm water so it is runny. Break up the chocolate and melt in a heatproof bowl above a small pan of simmering water. Beat in the 3 tablespoons of boiling water until thoroughly combined. Halve the cherries.

To assemble the puffs, carefully slice each piece of pastry in half, horizontally. Brush the bottom layer pieces with a little lemon icing, then spoon on some whipped cream and melted chocolate. Press a few cherry pieces into the chocolate and cream. Cover with the pastry tops and drizzle with melted chocolate and lemon icing.

Five ways with apples

260
Baked
Core apples and stuff with dried fruit soaked in brandy and unsalted butter. Place in an oven dish, cover loosely with foil and bake at 150°C for an hour, uncovering for the last 20 minutes.

261
Sauce
Peel and chop cooking apples, then cook in a little water until soft. Add sweeteners (honey, brown sugar, maple syrup) and spices (cinnamon, allspice, nutmeg, cloves) to taste.

262
Soup
Apples lend a subtle sweetness to soups made with root vegetables such as celeriac, carrots, parsnips or beetroot. Fry them with the vegetables, add vegetable stock and blend.

263
Salad
The classic Waldorf salad is made with apples, walnuts and celery tossed in mayonnaise, but apples can also work well with fennel, beetroot and cabbage. Apple juice can also be used in dressings, blended with oil and finely chopped shallots.

264
Juice
Apple and carrot juice is the classic 'starter' when experimenting with juicing. Try juicing a little ginger root with the mixture, or add a splash of freshly squeezed lemon juice.

265 Vegan raspberry muffins

Makes 12

Ingredients

- 250 ml soya milk
- 1 tablespoon apple cider vinegar
- 300 g plain flour
- 1 ½ teaspoons baking powder
- 1 teaspoon bicarbonate of soda
- ½ teaspoon salt
- 85 g sugar
- 90 ml unsweetened apple sauce
- 1 teaspoon vanilla esence
- 100 g raspberries

Preparation

Preheat the oven to 190°C. Grease a muffin tin or line with paper or silicone cases.

Mix the soya milk with the vinegar and leave to one side for five minutes to curdle. Sift the flour, baking powder, bicarbonate of soda and salt into a large mixing bowl, and stir in the sugar. Add the apple sauce and vanilla essence to the curdled soya milk, and then pour the wet ingredients over the dry ingredients and stir until just combined. Gently fold in the raspberries. Divide the mixture between the muffin cups and bake for 20 minutes.

266 Pear custard

Serves 4

Ingredients

- Butter, for greasing
- 4 ripe pears
- 175 g plain flour
- 175 g granulated sugar,
     plus 2 tablespoons
- 4 large eggs
- 475 ml single cream
- Maple syrup, to serve

Preparation

Preheat the oven to 190°C.

Peel, quarter and core the pears, and arrange them in the base of a greased baking dish.

In a large bowl, mix the flour and sugar together (reserving 2 tablespoons of the sugar), then beat in the eggs and the single cream. Pour over the pears and sprinkle with the reserved sugar. Bake for 45 minutes, until golden. Serve topped with a little maple syrup.

267 Blackberry and apple crumble

Serves 4

Ingredients

- 450 g cooking apples
- 300 g blackberries
- 60 g granulated sugar
- ½ teaspoon ground allspice
- 140 g plain flour
- 85 g unsalted butter
- 50 g chopped toasted hazelnuts
- 40 g brown sugar

Preparation

Preheat the oven to 190°C.

Peel, core and slice the apples, and arrange them in the base of a greased baking dish with the blackberries. Sprinkle on the sugar and allspice.

Put the flour into a large bowl, blend in the butter and then stir in the nuts and brown sugar. Cover the fruit with the crumble topping, pressing down gently to make a firm layer. Bake for 30 minutes, until golden and crisp.

268 Apple and almond cake

Serves 6

Ingredients

- 4 apples
- 25 g unsalted butter
- 2 tablespoons brown sugar
- 1 teaspoon ground cinnamon

For the cake

- 150 g unsalted butter
- 125 g sugar
- 2 medium eggs
- 1 teaspoon almond essence
- 75 g self-raising flour
- 75 g ground almonds

Preparation

Preheat the oven to 160°C. Grease a 20-cm baking tin and line the base with baking parchment.

Peel, core and slice the apples. Melt the butter in a frying pan, stir in the sugar and keep stirring until the mixture bubbles. Add the sliced apples and cinnamon and cook gently, turning occasionally, until tender and slightly caramelised. Remove from the heat.

For the cake, beat the butter and sugar together in a large bowl until light and fluffy, then gradually beat in the eggs and almond essence. Gently fold in the flour and ground almonds, and spoon the mixture into the prepared tin. Smooth the surface and arrange the cooked apples on top. Pour any juice left in the frying pan over the batter.

Bake for 45 minutes, using a skewer to check that it is cooked through. Before removing the cake from the pan, leave to cool for a few minutes.

Serve this cake warm with whipped cream or Greek yogurt.

Five ways with nuts

269

Breakfast energy

Enjoy an energising raw-food breakfast of hazelnuts and pecans, dates or dried apricots, sultanas and fresh seasonal fruit, chopped together and moistened with fruit juice or nut milk.

270

Nut milk

Make a dairy alternative by blending cashews, macadamias or almonds with cold water in a blender. Strain through muslin or a nut milk bag, and sweeten with maple syrup or agave nectar.

271

Spiced nuts

Toss whole, blanched almonds with a little vegetable oil, sprinkle with ground cumin and coriander, and bake for 10 minutes in a moderate oven until crisp.

272

Sweet treat

Coat pecans, macadamias and Brazil nuts with a mixture of beaten egg white, sugar and spices such as cinnamon, ground ginger or cloves, and bake at 150ºC for 45 minutes.

273

Pesto

Walnuts, cashews and pecans all work well for pestos – sticking to a single variety will give the best flavour. Use a blender or a pestle and mortar, and grind to a paste with basil, parsley or coriander and olive oil and sea salt.

274 Vegan vanilla cupcakes

Makes 12

Ingredients

- 1 teaspoon cider vinegar
- 250 ml soya milk
- 60 ml rapeseed oil
- 2 teaspoons vanilla essence
- 140 g caster sugar
- 200 g plain flour
- 2 tablespoons cornflour
- ¾ teaspoon baking powder
- ½ teaspoon bicarbonate of soda
- ½ teaspoon salt

For the icing

- 100 g margarine
- 280 g icing sugar
- ½ teaspoon vanilla essence
- 1 ½ tablespoons soya milk

Preparation

Preheat the oven to 180°C. Grease a cupcake tin or line with paper or silicone cases.

Mix the vinegar and soya milk together and set aside for five minutes to curdle. Stir in the oil, sugar and vanilla essence. Sift the flour, cornflour, baking powder, bicarbonate of soda and salt together. Combine the wet and dry ingredients and mix to a smooth batter. Divide the mixture between the paper cases in the cupcake tin and bake for 20 minutes, until cooked through and golden. Transfer to a wire rack to cool before icing.

To make the icing, cream all the ingredients together well. Use a spatula or a piping bag to ice the cakes.

275 Baked berry cheesecake

Serves 8

Ingredients

- 10 digestive biscuits
- 5 g unsalted butter
- 600 g cream cheese
- 2 tablespoons plain flour
- 175 g caster sugar
- 2 medium eggs plus 1 egg yolk
- 150 ml sour cream
- 2 to 3 drops vanilla essence
- 150 g mixed raspberries, blackberries or other berries

For the sauce

- 150 g mixed blackberries, raspberries, blueberries or other berries
- 2 tablespoons icing sugar

Preparation

Preheat the oven to 180°C.

Crush the biscuits and melt the butter. Mix the biscuit crumbs and butter together and spread over the base of a greased 20-cm loose-base baking tin, pressing down firmly. Bake for five minutes, then set aside.

Beat the cream cheese, flour, sugar, eggs and egg yolk, sour cream and vanilla essence together until well combined. Gently stir in the berries and pour over the cheesecake base. Smooth the top and bake for 45 minutes, until set. Leave to cool in the tin before turning out.

To make the sauce, rinse the berries and put them into a saucepan with the sugar. Warm gently, stirring occasionally until the berries collapse and release their juice. Push through a sieve and discard the pulp. Serve the sauce with the cheesecake as an optional extra!

276 Raspberry clafoutis
Serves 6

Ingredients
- 3 tablespoons plain flour
- Pinch salt
- 3 tablespoons sugar
- 3 medium eggs
- 300 ml milk
- 1 tablespoon oil
- 1 tablespoon unsalted butter, for greasing
- 225 g raspberries
- Icing sugar, to garnish

Preparation
Heat the oven to 180°C.

Put the flour, salt and sugar into a big bowl. In another bowl beat the eggs, milk and oil together, then beat into the other ingredients to make a smooth batter. Grease a deep 20-cm baking dish and line it with baking parchment. Put the raspberries in the dish and carefully pour over the batter.

Bake for 45 minutes, then reduce the oven temperature to 150°C and cook for a further 30 minutes. Test whether the clafoutis is cooked by inserting the tip of a knife or a skewer. It should come out clean. Remove from the oven and allow the clafoutis to stand for an hour and then serve straight from the dish, sprinkled with icing sugar.

Winter

Soups, salads, and appetizers

Mains and sides

Drinks and sweets

Fresh in Season ...

Parsnips

Giant parsnips are impressive to look at but can be woody inside – choose firm, medium-sized specimens for cooking or cut out the dense core. Peel, boil and mash them, or blanch and roast them, as you would potatoes.

Sweet potatoes

Look for medium-sized roots with good uniform colour and no soft spots. Sweet potatoes should be peeled and roasted or boiled – large ones are good baked in their skins and served with butter or vegan mayonnaise.

Celeriac

This large, dense root is a relative of celery and has a distinctive, subtle celery flavour. Don't worry about the lumpy exterior – just peel it with a potato peeler, cut it into chunks and try it boiled, roasted or mashed. Note that this vegetable is also sometimes called celery root.

Cauliflower

Look for cauliflowers with pure white 'curds' protected by crisp green outer leaves. They're not just for baking in cheese sauce – their subtle flavour works well with curries, or try individual florets deep-fried in tempura batter.

Red cabbage

Choose medium-sized, firm cabbages and peel away the outermost leaves before using. Grated red cabbage adds colour and texture to winter salads, and is also popular when baked slowly with apples and served as a side dish.

Kohlrabi

Also called turnip-rooted cabbage, there are green and purple varieties. Look for small young specimens that are crisp and tender – they can be grated or sliced and eaten raw, or stir-fried. More mature specimens are best steamed and then peeled.

Kale

Kale's dark green crinkly leaves can be cooked like cabbage (cut out any really tough-looking 'ribs'), but it is also good raw. Shred it finely, add a citrus salad dressing and use your hands to squash and squeeze the salad before serving.

Brussels sprouts

Look for small, firm buds without many yellow leaves. Remove one or two outer leaves and, if the base is thick, cut a cross in the bottom to help it cook more quickly. Boil until tender but not soggy, or shred and stir-fry.

277 Tomato and red lentil soup

Serves 4

Ingredients

- 2 onions
- Few sprigs fresh marjoram
- Small handful fresh parsley
- 2 tablespoons olive oil
- 1.2 litres vegetable stock
- 2 x 400 g tins chopped tomatoes
- 175 g red lentils
- Salt and freshly ground black pepper

Preparation

Peel the onions and chop them roughly. Strip the marjoram leaves away from the woody stems and chop them finely along with the parsley. In a large saucepan, fry the chopped onions in the olive oil until softened. Pour in the stock and add the chopped tomatoes and lentils.

Simmer, covered, for up to 40 minutes, until the lentils are completely soft. Leave to cool a little, transfer to a blender and blend until smooth. Return to the saucepan, reheat and stir in the fresh herbs. Season with salt and pepper before serving.

This attractive orange soup looks lovely topped with a pool of green pesto. Look for a brand that uses vegetarian cheese – or better still, make your own!

278 Parsnip and apple soup

Serves 4

Ingredients

- 800 g parsnips
- 1 large cooking apple
- 1 sprig fresh sage
- 25 g salted butter
- 1.2 litres vegetable stock
- 2 cloves
- 125 ml single cream
- Salt and freshly ground black pepper

Preparation

Peel the parsnips, and peel and core the apple. Chop both into small pieces. Finely chop the sage. In a large saucepan, fry the parsnips and apple in the butter until soft. Pour in the stock and add the sage and cloves. Simmer, covered, for 20 minutes. Leave to cool slightly and remove the clove before transferring to a blender and blending until smooth. Before reheating, stir in the single cream and season with salt and pepper. This smooth, comforting soup is best served with crusty bread.

279 Hummus with hot spices

Serves 4

Ingredients
- 1 x 400 g tin chickpeas
- 1 clove garlic
- 1 tablespoon tahini
- Juice ½ lemon
- 1 tablespoon olive oil
- ½ teaspoon dried chilli flakes
- ½ teaspoon ground cumin
- ½ teaspoon ground coriander
- Salt and freshly ground black pepper
- 1 teaspoon vegetable oil, for frying
- ½ teaspoon hot paprika

Preparation

Drain and rinse the chickpeas, and reserve a tablespoon of them. Peel and crush the garlic. Put the chickpeas in a blender and blend to a soft paste with the tahini, garlic, lemon juice, olive oil, chilli flakes, cumin and coriander. Taste and adjust the seasoning with salt and pepper, adding a little more oil, tahini or lemon juice according to taste if the mixture seems too thick.

Heat the vegetable oil in a frying pan and fry the reserved whole chickpeas for up to three minutes, turning frequently, until they begin to brown. To serve, transfer the hummus to a large shallow bowl and top with the whole chickpeas, a swirl of olive oil and a sprinkle of hot paprika.

280 Hot radicchio salad

Serves 4

Ingredients
- 1 blood orange
- 1 head radicchio
- 1 tablespoon olive oil
- 1 teaspoon caraway seeds
- 1 red chilli
- 1 small red onion
- 1 teaspoon cider vinegar
- 1 tablespoon red wine
- 1 tablespoon wholegrain mustard
- 1 teaspoon honey or maple syrup

Preparation

Grate the zest from the orange and squeeze out the juice. Cut the radicchio into quarters, discard the tough core and separate the leaves. Toss with the orange zest and juice, olive oil and caraway seeds. De-seed and finely chop the chilli. Peel and slice the onion, then marinate with the chopped chilli in a mixture of the cider vinegar, red wine, mustard and honey or maple syrup for at least 15 minutes, or until you are ready to serve the dish.

Stir-fry the radicchio and the onion mixture together in a large saucepan or wok on a high heat for five minutes, until the leaves are wilted and the flavours well combined.

281 Onion soup

Serves 4

Ingredients

- 900 g onions
- 50 g salted butter
- 2 tablespoons plain flour
- 1.2 litres vegetable stock
- 3 tablespoons sherry
- Soy sauce, to taste
- Salt and freshly ground black pepper

Preparation

Peel the onions and slice thinly into rings. In a large heavy pan, fry the onions gently in the butter for up to 20 minutes, until they are a rich, golden brown. Stir in the flour and gradually add the warm stock, stirring continuously. Stir in the sherry and simmer for 15 minutes. Taste and adjust the seasoning with soy sauce, salt and pepper. Serve with a bowl of finely shredded vegetarian cheese, so that people can help themselves, or with cheese on toast, cut into fingers.

282 Beetroot consommé

Serves 4

Ingredients

- 900 g raw beetroot
- 2 carrots
- 2 turnips
- 2 litres vegetable stock
- 2 teaspoons red wine vinegar
- Salt and freshly ground black pepper

Preparation

Peel the beetroots, carrots and turnips, and finely chop. Put them into a large saucepan with the stock, bring to the boil and simmer, covered, for 45 minutes, until the vegetables are soft.

Strain the soup through a sieve but take care not to press the vegetables – just drain off the clear liquid. If you push the vegetables through, you will end up with muddy consommé! Reheat and season to taste with the vinegar, salt and pepper.

283 Beetroot and fennel topping

Serves 4

Ingredients

- 3 beetroots
- 3 tablespoons olive oil
- Salt and freshly ground black pepper
- 1 fennel bulb
- 1 tablespoon balsamic vinegar
- 1 teaspoon fennel seeds

Preparation

Preheat the oven to 220°C.

Trim away the beetroot leaves but do not cut or peel the roots. Put the beetroots into a bowl and mix with half the olive oil and seasoning. Transfer to a large square of baking parchment, fold into a parcel and wrap the parcel in kitchen foil. Roast in the oven for up to 90 minutes, until the beetroot is tender.

Cut the fennel from top to bottom into 0.5-cm slices. Place in a bowl and toss with the remaining olive oil and balsamic vinegar. Transfer to a baking tray and cook for 20 minutes, until golden but not browned.

Allow the beetroots to cool a little, then rub off the skins under cold running water. Trim the ends, cut into small dice and place in a bowl. Chop the cooked fennel into small pieces and add to the beetroots. Crush the fennel seeds and stir into the mixture. Serve warm on blinis or as a side dish.

284 Buckwheat blinis

Makes 12

Ingredients

- 125 ml milk
- 5 g dried yeast
- 1 medium egg
- 75 g buckwheat or spelt flour
- Pinch salt
- Vegetable oil, for frying

Preparation

Warm the milk gently until it is tepid, and divide equally between two small bowls. Dissolve the yeast in one of the bowls of milk and put it in a warm place. Leave to stand for 45 minutes, until the yeast begins to work and bubbles appear on the surface of the mixture.

Separate the egg, beat the yolk into the second bowl of milk and then transfer both the milk mixtures to a large mixing bowl. Mix in the flour and salt, cover with a damp cloth and leave in a warm place for an hour. Then beat the egg white to stiff peaks and gently fold in.

Lightly oil a large, heavy frying pan and allow it to warm before dropping small spoonfuls of the blini mixture onto the hot surface. Cook gently for up to two minutes on each side, until puffy and golden.

285 Winter squash and sage topping

Serves 4

Ingredients

- 350 g winter squash: butternut squash, acorn squash or pumpkin
- Handful fresh sage
- Handful red chilli
- 2 tablespoons olive oil
- Salt and freshly ground black pepper
- 1 tablespoon vegetable oil, for frying

Preparation

Preheat the oven to 200°C.

Peel the squash and cut it into small cubes. Set aside a few sage leaves for a garnish and chop the rest finely. De-seed and chop the halved chilli finely.

Toss the squash pieces with the olive oil, salt and pepper, transfer to a baking tray and roast for up to 20 minutes, until tender and beginning to caramelise. Transfer the squash with the cooking oil to a large bowl and mix together with the chopped sage and chilli.

Heat the vegetable oil in a frying pan and very quickly fry the sage leaves until they begin to crisp – this only takes about 10 seconds. Remove from the pan with a slotted spoon and leave to cool on a sheet of kitchen towel.

Top blinis or toasted sourdough bread with a teaspoon or two of the warm squash mixture, and decorate each with a sage leaf.

286 Spinach and walnut pâté
Serves 4

Ingredients
- 450 g fresh leaf spinach
- 2 cloves garlic
- 85 g walnut pieces
- 1 teaspoon ground coriander
- 1 teaspoon cayenne pepper
- Small handful fresh parsley
- 1 tablespoon olive oil
- Juice ½ lemon
- Salt and freshly ground black pepper

Preparation
Wash the spinach and cook it in a little water for five minutes, until wilted. Drain and set aside to cool.

Peel and crush the garlic and put it into a food processor with the walnuts, coriander, cayenne, parsley and olive oil. Blend to a coarse paste.

When the spinach is cool enough to handle, chop it finely and squeeze out as much water as you can. Add it to the nut mixture in the food processor and blend again, adding lemon juice, salt and pepper to taste.

Pâtés look attractive served as quenelles (see photo). The technique involves passing a little of the mixture back and forth between two spoons to make the distinctive shape. It's a nice skill to learn and you can find helpful short videos demonstrating the technique on the internet.

287 Broccoli and macadamia salad

Serves 4

Ingredients

- 75 g tinned chickpeas
- 2 cloves garlic
- Juice and zest ½ lemon
- 3 tablespoons olive oil
- 75 ml white wine vinegar
- 2 heads broccoli
- 140 g whole macadamia nuts

Preparation

Drain and rinse the chickpeas. Peel the garlic cloves and crush them. Blend together the chickpeas, garlic, lemon zest, olive oil and vinegar, adding lemon juice as required to make a runny consistency.

Divide the broccoli into individual florets and cut from top to bottom into slices about 0.5-cm thick. Toss with the macadamia nuts, transfer to a large shallow bowl and top with the chickpea dressing.

288 Celeriac, apple and grape salad

Serves 4

Ingredients

- 1 celeriac
- 2 firm dessert apples
- 100 g walnut halves or pieces
- 200 g green seedless grapes
- Approximately 200 ml mayonnaise

Preparation

Peel the celeriac using a sharp knife to remove the knobbly brown outer layer. Cut the white flesh into thin slices and then into matchsticks. Blanch the celeriac in a large saucepan of boiling salted water for 30 seconds. Transfer to a colander and refresh under cold running water.

Slice the apples into matchsticks similar in size and shape to the celeriac pieces. Toast the walnut halves in a heavy dry saucepan for a few minutes. Halve the grapes. Pat the celeriac and apple dry with kitchen towel. Transfer to a bowl with the toasted walnuts and grapes, and stir in sufficient mayonnaise to coat all the fruit, nuts and vegetables.

289 Immune booster salad

Serves 4

Ingredients

- 100 g pearl barley
- 200 g wild rice
- 750 ml water
- Pinch salt
- 1 small red onion
- 55 g arame seaweed
- 1 tablespoon sultanas
- 1 tablespoon goji berries
- Juice ½ lemon
- 2 tablespoons flaxseed oil
- 1 tablespoon cider vinegar
- 55 g toasted flaked almonds
- 40 g toasted sesame seeds

This powerhouse of a dish is crammed with superfoods to provide a real boost on a cold, dark day. Cider vinegar, goji berries and sea vegetables add colour and texture to a dish of wild rice and barley grains.

Preparation

Soak the barley in cold water for one hour. Drain, and place in a large saucepan with the wild rice, water and salt. Bring to the boil, then reduce to a very low heat and cook for approximately 40 minutes, until all the water has been absorbed. Leave to cool, then fluff with a fork.

Peel and finely chop the onion. Soak the arame in warm water for 10 minutes, then drain and rinse. Soak the sultanas and goji berries in the lemon juice for 10 minutes. Drain, reserving the lemon juice.

Beat together the flaxseed oil, cider vinegar and reserved lemon juice. Combine all the salad ingredients together in a large mixing bowl, reserving a few toasted almond flakes for decoration.

290 Red cabbage, beetroot and radish salad

Serves 4

Ingredients

- 450 g red cabbage
- 1 tablespoon soy sauce
- 2 tablespoons cider vinegar
- 2 beetroots
- 8 radishes
- 1 orange
- 1 blood orange
- 2 tablespoons olive oil
- Salt and freshly ground black pepper

Preparation

Finely shred the cabbage and put it in a large mixing bowl with the soy sauce and cider vinegar. Use your hands to scrunch the cabbage and make sure it is well coated with the dressing. Peel and grate the beetroots, and grate the radishes. Zest one of the oranges, and reserve the zest. Then peel both oranges with a sharp knife to remove all white pith, and carefully cut into segments, avoiding the membranes that separate the segments. Gently combine all the ingredients and chill for a few minutes before serving.

Many winter vegetables do not have to be cooked. Using them raw is the best way to preserve their nutrients, colour and texture. Potatoes are the exception and must always be cooked before eating.

291 Roasted chestnut salad

Ingredients

- 200 g wheat berries
- 140 g roasted chestnuts
- 3 carrots
- 3 spring onions
- Small handful fresh mint
- 1 tablespoon soy sauce
- 3 tablespoons white wine vinegar
- 1 tablespoon olive oil
- 70 g raisins

Preparation

Put the wheat berries in a bowl, cover with water and soak overnight. Drain and rinse the wheat berries, then place in a large saucepan, cover with water and bring to the boil. Reduce the heat and simmer for one hour, until the wheat berries become tender and begin to break open. Drain.

Roughly chop the roasted chestnuts, grate the carrots, then finely chop the spring onions and mint. Beat the soy sauce, wine vinegar and olive oil together, then stir in the wheat berries. Add the chestnuts, grated carrots, chopped spring onions, raisins and mint, and toss well to combine. Serve immediately.

Wheat 'berries' are simply grains of whole wheat. They're rich in fibre and have a chewy texture.

Five ways with parsnips

292
Roasted

Roasting parsnips brings out their sweetness. Simply peel and slice or dice, toss in olive oil and cook at 200°C for up to 40 minutes until tender and beginning to caramelise. Add aromatic toasted fennel or caraway seeds or a drizzle of truffle oil to really bring out the flavour.

293
Mashed

Try mashing parsnips or a mixture of two or three different root vegetables, such as swede and potato. Enrich the taste with buttery roasted garlic, hot chilli oil or fresh pesto.

294
In a cake

Just like carrots and pumpkins, parsnips are surprisingly sweet and can be used to make muffins and cakes. Combinations featuring maple syrup, hazelnuts, ginger or lime all work well.

295
In a soup or sauce

The classic combination is parsnip and apple, but Indian spices like cumin and garam masala work well too. Add a few tablespoons of coconut milk and a little hot chilli powder to make a simple korma-style curry sauce.

296
Rösti

Peel and grate parsnips, mix with seasoned flour, spiced with a little paprika, turmeric or cumin, and pan fry in small patties.

297 Chestnut sausage rolls

Makes 12

Ingredients

- 1 onion
- 1 clove garlic
- 250 g tinned unsweetened chestnut purée or cooked mashed chestnuts
- 1 tablespoon tomato paste
- 1 tablespoon soy sauce
- 115 g fresh breadcrumbs
- 1 teaspoon dried thyme
- 1 pack ready-roll puff pastry sheets

Preparation

Preheat the oven to 190°C.

Peel the onion and finely chop. Peel and crush the garlic. Mix all the ingredients for the filling together thoroughly in a large bowl. Working on a floured board, cut the pastry into long strips about 5-cm wide. Make a line of filling about as thick as your little finger down the centre of each pastry strip. Dampen one long edge of the pastry with a little water, roll up and seal. Cut each long roll into mini rolls around 2.5-cm long. Transfer to a baking tray lined with baking parchment, leaving room for them to puff up, then bake for 15 minutes, until golden.

If you can't find cooked chestnuts in a supermarket near you, they can be bought online – or you can make these delicious rolls using the recipe for Mushroom and Sage Sausages on page 198.

298 Cranberry and pear chutney

Serves 4

Ingredients

- 1 small onion
- 1 pear
- 1 tablespoon red wine vinegar
- 1 tablespoon brandy
- 225 g fresh or frozen cranberries
- 55 g brown sugar
- ½ teaspoon mixed spice
- ½ teaspoon ground cinnamon
- ½ teaspoon ground ginger

Preparation

Peel the onion and chop it finely. Core the pear and chop it finely. Put the onion, pear, vinegar and brandy in a large saucepan and cook gently for 10 minutes, until the onion and pear have softened. Stir in the cranberries, sugar and spices and cook for a further 15 minutes or so, until the cranberries split and the liquid is reduced to a thick consistency. Leave to cool, then store in a jar in the fridge for up to two weeks.

This is perfect with a cheese board, as a thoughtful gift or to serve with snacks such as the Chestnut Sausage Rolls (opposite).

299 Crunchy seed balls

Serves 4

Ingredients

- 115 g sesame seeds
- 55 g pumpkin seeds
- 55 g sunflower seeds
- 2 teaspoons toasted sesame oil
- 2 teaspoons soy sauce
- 1 stick celery
- 3 teaspoons cider vinegar
- 1 tablespoon fruit chutney

Preparation

Put the sesame seeds into a dry, heavy saucepan and warm them gently. As soon as they begin to change colour, put them onto a cool plate to stop from cooking.

Put half of the sesame seeds and all of the remaining ingredients into a food processor and process until the mixture holds together. Form it into 20 walnut-sized balls, and roll in the remaining toasted sesame seeds to coat. Refrigerate for up to three hours to firm up before serving.

300 Crisp red and green salad
Serves 4

Ingredients
- 1 carrot
- 55 g celeriac
- Few sprigs fresh thyme
- Juice ½ lemon
- 2 tablespoons olive oil
- 250 g mixed crisp red and green salad
- 3 tablespoons raw edamame beans
- 2 tablespoons cress

Preparation
Peel the carrot and celeriac, and use a julienne peeler to cut long, thin strips (you can use a knife, but if you are making a lot of salads, buying a julienne peeler is a good investment). Strip the leaves off the woody stems of the thyme. Mix the lemon juice and olive oil together.

To assemble the salad, toss the salad leaves together with the carrot, celeriac, edamame and thyme. Dress with the olive oil and lemon juice, and garnish with the cress.

Edamame are raw soya beans. They are available frozen, and it's handy to have a bag in the freezer, as they are an exceptional source of protein for vegetarians. Thaw a handful by putting them into a sieve and pouring over a kettle of boiling water. Refresh them under cold running water if you want to use them cold.

301 Kohlrabi and sweet potato pancakes

Serves 4

Ingredients

- 1 small kohlrabi
- 1 sweet potato
- 1 sprig fresh thyme
- 3 tablespoons gram (chickpea) flour
- Salt and freshly ground black pepper
- 1 medium egg
- Vegetable oil, for frying

Preparation

Peel the kohlrabi and sweet potato, and grate coarsely. Strip the thyme leaves from the woody stems and chop them finely. Transfer the grated vegetables to a large bowl and stir in the fresh thyme, gram flour and seasoning. Beat the egg and stir it into the mixture. Heat the oil in a heavy frying pan. Drop teaspoons of the mixture onto the hot surface, flatten into small cakes and cook for up to three minutes on each side, until crisp and golden. Serve immediately, with a fruity chutney or relish.

Kohlrabi is an under-used vegetable with a pleasant nutty flavour that marries beautifully with sweet potatoes. Both have a soft texture that contrasts with the crispy outer layer of these patties.

302 Brown rice salad with dates and pomegranate

Serves 4

Ingredients

- 150 g brown rice
- 4 dried, pitted dates
- 4 spring onions
- 1 teaspoon fennel seeds
- 1 teaspoon cumin seeds
- 2 tablespoons cashew nuts
- 2 tablespoons fresh pomegranate seeds
- 1 lemon
- 3 tablespoons olive oil

Preparation

Put the rice in a large saucepan of water, bring to the boil, reduce to a low heat and simmer for 40 minutes, until tender. Drain and rinse with cold water.

Chop the dates and slice the spring onions into fine rings. Crush the fennel and cumin seeds with a pestle and mortar or a rolling pin. Toast the cashews in a dry, heavy-bottomed saucepan until they begin to colour. Zest and juice the lemon.

Combine all the ingredients, cover and chill for at least 30 minutes to allow the flavours to develop.

303 Spiced winter pickle

Serves 4

Ingredients

- 1 large cauliflower
- 3 onions
- 3 carrots
- 1 cucumber
- 1 red pepper
- 200 g fine green beans
- 100 g salt
- 70 g plain flour
- 2 teaspoons curry powder
- 2 teaspoons ground turmeric
- 2 teaspoons mustard powder
- 2 teaspoons ground ginger
- 1 litre white wine vinegar
- 150 g granulated sugar

Preparation

Trim the cauliflower and break it into small florets. Peel and dice the onions. Peel and slice the carrots. Peel, de-seed and slice the cucumber. De-seed the red pepper and slice into fine strips. Trim the beans and chop into 2.5-cm pieces. Put all the prepared vegetables into a large mixing bowl and toss with the salt. Transfer to a colander, cover and leave in the kitchen sink for 12 hours or overnight. Then wash the vegetables well in several changes of water and put them back into the colander to drain thoroughly.

Put the flour and spices into a very large saucepan or preserving pan and heat them gently, stirring constantly. Gradually pour in the vinegar, stirring all the time to make sure no lumps are formed. Stir in the sugar and bring to the boil – the mixture should thicken. Put the prepared vegetables into the pan, stir well to combine with the spicy sauce and cook for a further three minutes, until all the vegetables are hot.

Pour into sterilised jars and seal immediately. Leave for four weeks before using.

304 Warm red cabbage salad

Serves 4

Ingredients

- 1 small red cabbage
- 2 shallots
- 1 green apple
- 2 spring onions
- 2 to 3 sprigs fresh thyme
- 2 tablespoons olive oil
- 55 g walnuts
- 85 g soft rindless goat's cheese

Preparation

Core and shred the cabbage. Peel and finely slice the shallots. Core and thinly slice the apple. Chop the spring onions, leaving the green parts in pieces about 2.5-cm long. Strip the leaves off the woody stems of the thyme.

Heat the oil in a large saucepan or wok and stir-fry the cabbage, shallots and walnuts for up to six minutes, until the shallots are soft and the cabbage is cooked but still crisp. Add the apple slices to the cabbage mixture, stir-frying for a further minute or two, until they are warmed through. Transfer to a serving dish and dress with the thyme leaves and the spring onions. Tuck in small pieces of crumbled goat's cheese and serve while the cabbage is still warm.

If not using the prepared apple immediately, you can put it in a bowl of water with the juice of half a lemon, to prevent browning. Remember to drain the slices well before using.

305 Baked parsnips with sour cream

Serves 4

Ingredients

- 450 g parsnips
- 1 onion
- 2 cloves garlic
- 2 tablespoons vegetable oil
- 300 ml vegetable stock
- ½ teaspoon mustard
- ½ teaspoon paprika
- 150 ml sour cream
- 50 g fresh breadcrumbs
- 25 g Cheddar cheese

Preparation

Preheat the oven to 200°C.

Peel the parsnips and slice them about 0.5-cm thick. Peel and finely chop the onion. Peel and crush the garlic. Warm the oil in a large saucepan and gently fry the onion for about five minutes, until it is soft and beginning to brown. Add the parsnips and fry for a further five minutes, until they begin to colour and soften. Stir in the garlic and cook for a minute or two before adding the stock, mustard and paprika. Bring to the boil, then turn down the heat and simmer, covered, for 15 minutes.

Remove the pan from the heat and leave to cool slightly before stirring in the sour cream. Transfer to a baking dish, top with the breadcrumbs and cheese, and then bake until crisp and golden, around 20 minutes.

306 Red cabbage with toasted pecans

Serves 4

Ingredients

- 55 g pecans
- 1 small red cabbage
- 1 red onion
- 1 shallot
- 2 tablespoons orange juice
- 1 tablespoon red wine vinegar
- 2 tablespoons olive oil

Preparation

Toast the pecans in a dry, heavy-bottomed saucepan for up to three minutes, until they begin to brown. As soon as they start to change colour, remove the pan from the heat and turn the nuts onto a plate to stop them from cooking any further. Finely shred the cabbage, discarding the woody centre. Peel and slice the onion. Peel and finely slice the shallot. Beat the orange juice, shallot and vinegar together.

Heat the oil in a large saucepan or wok, and stir-fry the cabbage and red onions for three minutes, until hot but still quite firm. Stir in the pecans and dressing, toss to combine and heat through for a further minute before serving.

307 Stir-fried vegetable parcels with lemon cream

Serves 4

Ingredients
- 1 pack ready-made filo pastry
- 25 g salted butter
- 300 g mixed vegetables: baby sweetcorn, broccoli florets, fine green beans, peppers, asparagus, carrots
- 1 tablespoon vegetable oil

For the sauce
- 1 clove garlic
- 1 tablespoon salted butter
- 125 ml light vegetable stock
- 125 ml single cream
- 1 tablespoon cornflour
- 3 tablespoons lemon juice
- Freshly ground black pepper

Preparation
Preheat the oven to 180°C. Cut 12 large circles from the pastry sheets using a dinner plate as a guide. Melt the butter and brush four of the pastry circles. Cover each with another piece of pastry and repeat to make four stacks of three pastry sheets. Put the pastry on a baking tray lined with baking parchment and put a little crumpled baking parchment at the centre of each circle. Carefully fold the edges of the pastry up around the parchment to create open pastry cases. Bake for up to eight minutes, until crisp and golden. Allow the pastry cases to cool before carefully removing the parchment.

Make the sauce. Peel and crush the garlic and fry it gently in the butter for a minute. Stir in the stock and single cream. Bring the mixture to boiling point, then reduce the heat and simmer for three minutes. Mix the cornflour with the lemon juice and beat this into the cream, stirring to prevent any lumps. Cook for a further two minutes, until the mixture is thickening, and season with black pepper.

Peel and chop the vegetables into bite-sized pieces and stir-fry in the oil for five minutes until cooked through but still crisp. Arrange the hot cooked vegetables in and on top of the pastry cases. Reheat the lemon cream sauce and top each serving with a little sauce.

308 Cauliflower with tahini dressing

Serves 4

Ingredients
- 1 cauliflower
- 2 teaspoons cumin seeds

For the dressing
- Small handful fresh parsley
- Few sprigs fresh mint
- 2 teaspoons white wine vinegar
- 1 tablespoon light tahini
- Juice 1 lemon
- Salt and freshly ground black pepper

Preparation
Trim the cauliflower, separate it into small florets and boil in lightly salted water for 10 minutes. Toast the cumin seeds in a dry, heavy-bottomed saucepan until they release their aroma. Remove from the hot pan and set aside.

To make the dressing, finely chop the fresh herbs. Beat together the wine vinegar, tahini, lemon juice, herbs and seasoning.

Drain the cauliflower and place in a warmed serving dish. Pour over the dressing, sprinkle with the toasted cumin seeds and serve immediately.

309 Cauliflower, leek and haricot bean bake

Serves 4

Ingredients
- 2 leeks
- 1 orange pepper
- ½ small cauliflower
- 2 tablespoons vegetable oil
- ½ teaspoon smoked paprika
- ½ x 400 g tin haricot beans
- 125 ml crème fraîche
- 150 ml plain yogurt
- 25 g smoked Cheddar cheese

Preparation
Preheat the oven to 200°C.

Trim and finely slice the leeks De-seed and slice the pepper, divide the cauliflower into florets. In a large saucepan or wok, stir-fry the vegetables together with the vegetable oil and smoked paprika for five minutes.

Drain and rinse the beans, and mix together with the vegetables, crème fraîche and yogurt. Transfer to a shallow baking dish. Grate the cheese over the top and bake for 15 to 20 minutes, until golden and bubbling.

310 Creamy Jerusalem artichokes with mushrooms

Serves 4

Ingredients

- 250 g Jerusalem artichokes
- 200 g button mushrooms
- 2 tablespoons vegetable oil
- 3 cloves garlic
- 1 teaspoon dried rosemary
- 1 teaspoon dried thyme
- 120 ml dry white wine
- 60 ml double cream

Preparation

Preheat the oven to 180°C.

Scrub the Jerusalem artichokes and slice them finely. Wipe and slice the mushrooms.

Fry the Jerusalem artichokes and mushrooms gently in the oil for five minutes, until the mushrooms have released their juices and the mixture is no longer wet. Peel and crush the garlic, add to the pan and cook for a further minute.

Stir in the herbs and wine and simmer, covered, for five minutes, until the Jerusalem artichokes are tender. Stir in the cream and heat through before serving.

Jerusalem artichokes are an often overlooked member of the winter root family, and are a great alternative to potatoes or parsnips, with a nutty and sweet flavour. This rich and velvety dish would go perfectly with some green beans or cabbage as a hearty main, or could be served alongside a nut loaf as part of a winter dinner party spread.

311 Sweetcorn fritters

Serves 4

Ingredients

- 1 x 330 g tin sweetcorn
- 4 spring onions
- 1 medium egg
- 2 tablespoons plain flour
- Salt and freshly ground black pepper
- Vegetable oil, for frying

Preparation

Drain the sweetcorn and put it into a large mixing bowl. Trim and chop the spring onions and add them to the sweetcorn. Separate the egg into white and yolk. Mix the yolk, flour and seasoning into the sweetcorn. Beat the egg white into soft peaks and gently fold it into the sweetcorn mixture.

Heat a little oil in a frying pan and fry a tablespoon of the mixture, turning once, until crisp and golden on both sides. Repeat with the remaining batter, frying in batches. Serve immediately.

Add some finely chopped fresh chillies to these fritters to warm you up on a cold day. When being cooked, the sweetcorn can spit and pop, so it's best to wear an apron and be prepared for some splashes.

312 Turkish fried potatoes

Serves 4

Ingredients

- 450 g potatoes
- 2 onions
- 2 spring onions
- Handful fresh parsley
- ½ tablespoon olive oil
- 1 tablespoon tomato pureé
- ½ teaspoon hot paprika
- Juice ½ lemon
- Salt and freshly ground black pepper

Preparation

Peel the potatoes, cut them into chunks if they are large and boil them in salted water, until cooked through but not disintegrating. When cool enough to handle, cut them into bite-sized pieces. Peel and roughly chop the onion, and trim and chop the spring onions. Chop the fresh parsley.

Warm the oil in a large saucepan and gently fry the onions and spring onions, until soft and translucent. Stir in the tomato paste and paprika, and mix the potatoes in thoroughly. Season, and cook until all the sauce has been absorbed by the potatoes. Dress the dish with lemon juice and parsley and serve hot or cold.

313 Honey-glazed root vegetable ribbons

Serves 4

Ingredients

- 2 parsnips
- 4 carrots
- 1 orange
- 3 tablespoons honey
- 1 tablespoon sesame oil
- 1 tablespoon olive oil
- 2 tablespoons sesame seeds

Preparation

Preheat the oven to 190°C.

Peel the parsnips and carrots and slice them lengthways as thinly as you can. Parboil them in a large saucepan of boiling salted water for five minutes. Slice one half of the orange into thin rounds, and set aside. Zest and juice the other half of the orange. Warm the honey in a small pan. Drain the parsnips and carrots, and transfer to a large bowl. Toss with the honey, sesame oil, olive oil, sesame seeds and orange juice and zest. Put the mixture in a shallow baking dish and cook in the oven for up to 20 minutes, until just brown. Serve decorated with the reserved orange slices.

314 Baked kale in creamy onion sauce

Serves 4

Ingredients
- 1.5 kg curly kale
- 5 onions
- 1 potato
- 2 cloves garlic
- 1 bay leaf
- 4 cloves
- 1 teaspoon yeast extract
- 3 vegetable stock cubes
- 900 ml milk or soya milk
- Salt and freshly ground black pepper
- 2 tablespoons sunflower seeds

Preparation

Preheat the oven to 190°C.

Chop the kale and discard any tough stems. Cook in a large saucepan of boiling water for 10 minutes. Peel and chop the onions. Peel the potato and cut into small dice. Bruise the garlic (crush it with the flat side of a knife) but keep the cloves whole. Put the chopped onion and potato, garlic, bay leaf, cloves, yeast extract, stock cubes and milk in a large saucepan and simmer, covered, for 30 minutes, until the potatoes and onions are very soft. Remove the cloves, garlic and bay leaf, and blend until smooth. Taste and season with salt and pepper.

Drain the kale and arrange it in a baking dish. Pour the sauce over, sprinkle with the sunflower seeds and then bake for 20 minutes, until golden and bubbling.

315 Spicy tomato sauce

Serves 4

Ingredients
- 1 onion
- 4 cloves garlic
- 1 tablespoon olive oil
- 2 x 400 g tins chopped tomatoes
- 1 teaspoon cinnamon
- 1 tablespoon apple cider
- 1 tablespoon lemon juice
- Salt and freshly ground black pepper

Preparation

Peel and finely chop the onion. Peel and crush the garlic. Heat the oil in a saucepan and gently fry the onion until soft and translucent. Stir in the garlic and cook for another minute, then add the chopped tomatoes, cinnamon, apple cider and lemon juice. Simmer for 10 minutes and season to taste with salt and pepper. This sauce would be the perfect companion served hot with the Stuffed Cabbage Leaves on page 266.

316 Kale and ginger stir-fry

Serves 4

Ingredients
- 900 g kale, preferably cavolo nero
- 2.5 cm ginger root
- 1 tablespoon fennel seeds
- 6 tablespoons olive oil
- ½ teaspoon dried red chilli flakes
- Salt and freshly ground black pepper

Preparation
Wash the kale and trim away the thickest stems. Shred the leaves. Grate the ginger.

Roast the fennel seeds for one minute in a dry frying pan or wok. Then add the oil, grated ginger, chilli flakes and seasoning to the pan and cook for up to three minutes. Add the shredded kale and stir-fry for five minutes. Season to taste with salt and freshly ground black pepper.

Cavolo nero is a dark-leaved variety of kale, traditionally an important source of fresh vitamins in the depths of winter as it survived very cold weather!

317 Curly kale with caramelised shallots

Serves 4

Ingredients
- 900 g curly kale
- 10 shallots
- 4 tablespoons olive oil
- Salt and freshly ground black pepper

Preparation
Wash and shred the kale. Cook in a large saucepan of boiling water for five minutes, then drain. Peel and finely slice the shallots. In a large saucepan, fry the shallots in the olive oil until meltingly soft and golden brown. Stir in the cooked kale and toss together to spread the flavoured oil and shallots through the dish. Stir-fry for up to three minutes, until warmed through. Season to taste with salt and freshly ground black pepper.

318 Broccoli and orange stir-fry

Serves 4

Ingredients

- 2 tablespoons sunflower seeds
- 1 tablespoon soy sauce
- 4 oranges
- 750 g broccoli
- 3 tablespoons rapeseed oil
- 1 teaspoon fennel seeds
- Salt and freshly ground black pepper

Preparation

Toast the sunflower seeds in a heavy-bottomed saucepan for three minutes. Splash the soy sauce into the pan and stir quickly to coat the seeds before the liquid sizzles away. Remove from the heat. Grate the zest from two of the oranges and squeeze out the juice. Cut the peel off the other two oranges and cut them into segments. Cut the broccoli into bite-sized florets. Chop up the stems too, discarding any particularly thick and woody pieces.

Heat the oil in a large saucepan or wok, and stir-fry the broccoli with the orange zest and fennel seeds for five minutes. Reduce the heat and pour in the orange juice. Cook gently for a further eight minutes or so, until the broccoli is just tender. Season with salt and pepper, and toss the orange segments and sunflower seeds through the broccoli before serving.

319 Pasta arrabbiata with broccoli

Serves 4

Ingredients

- 450 g broccoli
- 225 g dried wholewheat pasta
- 1 red pepper
- 1 red chilli
- 2 cloves garlic
- 4 tablespoons olive oil
- 1 teaspoon freshly ground black pepper
- Chilli oil, optional

Preparation

Trim the broccoli into florets and cook in boiling water until just tender. Cook the pasta in salted boiling water until just tender, and drain.

De-seed and chop the pepper and chilli. Peel and chop the garlic. Heat the olive oil in a large saucepan. Add the chilli, red pepper, garlic and black pepper, and cook for one minute. Add the drained, cooked broccoli florets and pasta, toss together thoroughly and continue to cook until the dish is piping hot. Dress with a little chilli oil to serve.

Five ways with cabbage

320
Raw
Shred the leaves and let them wilt in a marinade of cider vinegar, some flavourful oil (such as walnut), a little sweetener (honey or maple syrup) and a dash of mustard or soy sauce.

321
Stir-fried
Sizzle some finely chopped garlic or ginger, or aromatic seeds such as cumin, fennel or caraway in a wok before adding shredded cabbage leaves. Fry until soft and add a splash of citrus juice.

322
Stuffed
Blanch the leaves first to make them more pliable, and make sure the filling is strongly flavoured, as you will only get a little taste in each bite. Steam the parcels or bake in a sauce until tender.

323
Deep-fried
The crispy seaweed served in Chinese restaurants is actually deep-fried shredded cabbage. Dry the leaves well before immersing them in hot oil for a few seconds in small batches. Drain on kitchen towel before seasoning with salt and sugar.

324
Juiced
Cabbage juice is rich in nutrients, but bitter-tasting, so dilute it with the juice of apples, oranges, carrots or pomegranates, or add some fresh mint as you feed it through the juicer.

325 Sweet potato, parsnip and carrot tagine

Serves 4

Ingredients
- 250 g sweet potatoes
- 250 g parsnips
- 250 g baby carrots
- 6 shallots
- 2.5 cm ginger root
- 2 tablespoons olive oil
- 500 ml vegetable stock
- 1 tablespoon honey or maple syrup
- 1 cinnamon stick
- 100 g pitted prunes
- Salt and freshly ground black pepper

Preparation
Preheat the oven to 180°C.

Peel the sweet potatoes and parsnips and chop them into large pieces. Peel the carrots, peel and halve the shallots, and peel and mince or finely chop the ginger.

Heat a flameproof casserole dish on the stove, and cook the shallots in the oil until softened. Stir in the sweet potatoes, carrots and parsnips and cook, stirring occasionally, for 10 minutes. Pour in the stock and add the honey or maple syrup, ginger, cinnamon stick, prunes, and salt and pepper. Cover and transfer to the oven. Cook for 30 minutes, stir the mixture and return to the oven, uncovered, for a further 15 minutes. Serve over warm rice or couscous.

326 Shredded greens with pomegranate

Serves 4

Ingredients
- 1.8 kg greens: kale, green cabbage or spring greens
- 1 tablespoon rapeseed oil
- 55 g pomegranate seeds

For the dressing
- 1 orange
- 7 g preserved stem ginger in syrup
- 2 tablespoons maple syrup
- 2 tablespoons olive oil
- 1 tablespoon white wine vinegar

Preparation
Make the dressing first. Juice the orange and finely chop the preserved stem ginger. Beat the juice together with the maple syrup, olive oil, ginger and vinegar.

Trim and shred the greens. Heat the rapeseed oil in a large saucepan or wok and stir-fry the greens for four minutes, until bright green and wilting. Toss the dressing through and serve immediately, topping each serving with pomegranate seeds.

327 Squash and sweet potato lasagne

Serves 4

Ingredients

- 900 g butternut squash
- 450 g sweet potatoes
- 2 onions
- 1 tablespoon olive oil
- 1 litre milk
- ¼ teaspoon nutmeg
- 1 bay leaf
- 40 g plain flour
- 140 g vegetarian Parmesan-style cheese
- Salt and freshly ground black pepper
- 1 pack lasagne sheets
- 140 g mozzarella cheese

Preparation

Preheat the oven to 230°C. Peel and chop the squash and sweet potato into bite-sized pieces. Peel and coarsely chop one of the onions. Put these into a bowl and toss with the olive oil to coat all of the pieces. Tip the vegetables onto a baking tray and roast for 30 minutes, until tender. Turn the oven down to 190°C.

Peel and roughly chop the other onion. Place in a saucepan with the milk, nutmeg and bay leaf. Heat to a simmer, remove from the heat and leave to infuse for 15 minutes. Strain and discard the solids. Return the milk to the pan and beat in the flour. Cook over a medium heat for around 10 minutes, until the mixture thickens, then stir in the Parmesan-style cheese and season.

Spread a quarter of the cheese sauce mixture into the base of a rectangular dish. Cover with a layer of noodles, then half of the roasted vegetables. Slice the mozzarella and use a third of it to cover the vegetables. Pour a third of the remaining sauce over the top. Layer again with pasta, the remaining vegetables, half the remaining mozzarella and half the remaining sauce. Cover with a final layer of pasta, then the last of the sauce and mozzarella.

Cover the dish with kitchen foil and bake for 20 minutes. Remove the foil and bake for a further 20 minutes, until the top of the lasagne is golden and bubbling.

328 Brussels sprouts with sherry-soaked cranberries

Serves 4

Ingredients

- 25 g dried cranberries
- 175 ml sweet sherry
- 40 g pistachios in shells
- ½ shallot
- 1 tablespoon sherry vinegar
- 1 teaspoon wholegrain mustard
- 1 tablespoon olive oil
- 1.8 kg Brussels sprouts
- 1 tablespoon rapeseed oil
- Salt and freshly ground black pepper

Preparation

Put the dried cranberries in a small saucepan with the sherry and bring to the boil. Turn to the lowest heat available and cook for 10 minutes. Set aside to cool to room temperature.

Shell the pistachios. Peel and finely chop the shallot, then make a dressing by beating together the sherry vinegar, mustard, olive oil and shallot. Cut the bottoms off the Brussels sprouts and separate them into individual leaves. Heat the rapeseed oil in a large saucepan or wok and stir-fry the Brussels sprouts leaves on a high heat for up to three minutes, moving them around constantly, until some of the leaves start to show brown patches.

Toss the dressing through the hot leaves, season and serve immediately, garnishing each serving with cranberries, their remaining soaking liquid and whole pistachios.

329 Saffron-spiced cauliflower
Serves 4

Ingredients

- 75 g sultanas
- Juice 1 orange
- 4 tablespoons olive oil
- Pinch saffron strands
- 1 cauliflower
- 1 onion
- 3 cloves garlic
- 1 teaspoon white wine vinegar
- 1 teaspoon paprika
- Salt and freshly ground black pepper
- Few springs fresh coriander

Preparation

Put the sultanas and orange juice in a small bowl and leave to soak. Put half of the olive oil into a small bowl with the saffron and leave to infuse. Trim the cauliflower and divide into florets. Blanch in a pan of boiling water for up to three minutes, until just tender. Drain and set aside.

Peel and finely chop the onion and garlic. In a large saucepan, fry the onion in the remaining oil until soft, then add the garlic and cauliflower. Cook for a further three minutes, then reduce the heat, sprinkle the paprika into the mixture and pour in the saffron and the oil. Stir thoroughly to coat the vegetables, then add the vinegar and cook for another three minutes. Finally, add the sultanas and orange juice. Stir to combine and continue to cook until the liquid is reduced. Season to taste with salt and pepper and garnish with fresh coriander before serving.

330 Trofie pasta with pesto

Serves 4

Ingredients

- 350 g dried trofie pasta
- 250 g baby new potatoes
- 100 g fine green beans, trimmed
- 4 tablespoons sage pesto (see page 270)
- Grated vegetarian cheese, to serve

Preparation

Peel the potatoes and boil, with the pasta, in a large saucepan of salted water for five minutes. Trim the beans and cut them into short pieces. Add these to the pan and continue to boil for a further five minutes, until the potatoes are cooked and the pasta is al dente. Drain the pasta, potatoes and beans, and return to the pan. Stir in the sage pesto. Serve with a bowl of grated cheese so that everybody can help themselves.

This is a classic combination that is loved in the Genoa region of Italy. Trofie pasta is said to resemble pigs' tails. Sometimes it is made with chestnut flour, so use this if you can find it, although other pasta would work in this dish too.

331 Leek and apple pilaf

Serves 4

Ingredients

- 1 leek
- 150 g brown rice
- 300 ml vegetable stock
- 250 ml apple juice or cider
- 1 dessert apple
- 70 g hazelnuts

Preparation

Trim the leek and slice it thinly. Mix together the rice, chopped leek, vegetable stock and apple juice or cider in a medium-sized saucepan. Bring to the boil, reduce the heat to the lowest possible setting, cover the pan and cook without stirring for 40 minutes.

Peel, core and finely chop the apple. Sprinkle the apple pieces on top of the rice, replace the lid of the pan and continue to cook for up to 10 minutes more, until the rice is tender and the liquid has been absorbed. Remove from the heat and leave to stand, covered, for five minutes before fluffing with a fork. Chop the hazelnuts and sprinkle them over the top of the dish before serving.

332 Stroganoff potatoes

Serves 4

Ingredients

- 4 baking potatoes
- 55 g button mushrooms
- 2 onions
- 15 cm piece kombu seaweed, optional
- 2 tablespoons olive oil
- 115 g firm tofu
- 2 tablespoons red wine vinegar
- 2 tablespoons tahini
- 2 tablespoons soy sauce
- 2 tablespoons arrowroot powder

Preparation

Preheat the oven to 200°C. Scrub the potatoes and prick the skins with a fork. Bake for approximately one hour, depending on their size, until the skins are crisp and the flesh is soft all the way through.

Wipe and trim the button mushrooms. Peel and chop the onion. Put the kombu (if using) into a saucepan with 475 ml of water, bring to the boil, cover and simmer for 10 minutes. Remove the kombu and set aside to dry.

Warm the oil in a large saucepan and gently fry the onions and mushrooms until the mushrooms begin to release their juices. Add half the kombu stock (save the rest to add to another soup or stew). Drain and press the tofu, and cut it into bite-sized pieces. Gently stir the tofu into the pan, cover and simmer on a very low heat for 20 minutes.

Mix the vinegar, tahini, soy sauce and arrowroot together, stir into the stroganoff and simmer for a further three minutes, until the sauce thickens.

Cut the baked potatoes in half and divide the stroganoff mixture between them.

Kombu is a sea vegetable that adds a rich savoury taste to vegetarian dishes. It can be used more than once to make stock in this way – allow it to dry out between uses.

333 Spinach roulade

Serves 4

Ingredients

- 200 g cooked spinach
- 115 g onion
- 4 medium eggs
- 115 g vegetarian Parmesan-style cheese
- 25 g salted butter
- 25 g plain flour
- 150 ml milk
- 175 g cream cheese
- Salt and freshly ground black pepper
- Pinch nutmeg

Preparation

Preheat the oven to 190°C. Grease and line a 33 x 23-cm Swiss roll tin with baking parchment.

To make the filling, first finely chop the spinach and onion. Separate the eggs. Grate the Parmesan-style cheese finely. In a large, heavy-bottomed saucepan, melt the butter. Stir in the flour and cook for a minute, then gradually stir in the milk. As the sauce thickens, remove a tablespoon of the mixture and reserve. Mix in the onion, cook for three minutes, then stir in the cream cheese until all the ingredients are combined. Season with nutmeg, salt and pepper and set aside.

To make the roulade, put the spinach into a food processor with the egg yolks and reserved sauce, season with salt and pepper and blend briefly until well mixed. Transfer to a large mixing bowl. In a separate bowl, beat the egg whites until they form stiff peaks and then gently fold them into the spinach mixture. Spoon the mixture into the tin and smooth it out. Bake for 15 minutes until risen and springy to touch.

Cover your work surface with a large sheet of baking parchment, sprinkled with the Parmesan-style cheese. While the roulade is still hot, turn it out of the tin onto the baking parchment and slowly roll up. When you are ready to serve, carefully unroll the roulade, and spread the filling over it. Re-roll and transfer to a serving plate. Serve warm or cold with Spicy Tomato Sauce (see page 249.)

334 Chestnut and sweet potato loaf

Serves 4

Ingredients

- 2 onions
- 2 cloves garlic
- 1 tablespoon olive oil
- 3 sweet potatoes
- 55 g salted butter
- 450 g fresh spinach
- 1 teaspoon ground nutmeg
- Sprig fresh rosemary
- 225 g roasted chestnuts
- 55 g walnuts
- 1 medium egg
- 115 g fresh breadcrumbs
- 1 tablespoon sun-dried
  tomato paste

Preparation

Preheat the oven to 180°C. Grease a 450-g loaf tin.

Peel and dice the onions, and peel and chop the garlic. Fry the onions in the olive oil until soft, add the garlic and continue to cook for a further minute or two. Remove from the heat. Peel the sweet potatoes and chop into small chunks. Cook in boiling water until tender, drain and mash with half of the butter. Cook the spinach in a large saucepan with a little water until wilted. Drain, cool slightly, then finely chop. Mix in the remaining butter and ground nutmeg. Strip the rosemary leaves from the woody stems and finely chop. Peel the chestnuts, and roughly chop the chestnuts and walnuts. Beat the egg. Mix together the breadcrumbs, chestnuts, walnuts, sun-dried tomato paste, chopped rosemary and egg. Add the cooked onions and garlic, and the mashed sweet potato, and mix well.

Put half of the nut roast mixture into the prepared loaf tin, and cover it with the cooked, chopped spinach. Put the remaining nut roast mixture on top, smooth the surface and cover with kitchen foil. Bake for 30 minutes, then remove the foil and return to the oven for a further 10 minutes to brown. Leave to stand in the tin for 10 minutes before turning out.

Look for vacuum-packed or frozen chestnuts if you can find them, as they are easy to use and keep well.

335 Baked squash with spiced couscous

Serves 4

Ingredients

- 2 small acorn squash (or other small winter squash)
- 2 tablespoons olive oil
- 200 g couscous
- Pinch saffron strands
- 25 g dried cherries
- 55 g pistachios
- 1 teaspoon harissa paste
- 1 teaspoon ras-el-hanout, optional
- Small handful fresh coriander
- Melted butter, to serve

Preparation

Preheat the oven to 200°C.

Cut the tops off the squashes, scoop out the seeds and brush the insides with olive oil. Put on a baking tray and roast for up to 40 minutes (depending on size of squash) until tender. Put the couscous in a shallow bowl with the saffron threads and pour over 225 ml of boiling water. Leave for 15 minutes until the water is absorbed, then fluff the couscous gently with a fork and transfer to a large mixing bowl. Mix in the dried cherries, pistachios, harissa paste and ras-el-hanout (if using). Finely chop the coriander and stir into the stuffing mix. Fill the squashes with the stuffing and return to the oven for a further 10 minutes. Spoon a little melted butter on top before serving.

Ras-el-hanout is an aromatic Moroccan spice blend that includes dried rose petals. Meaning 'head of the shop' in Arabic, the blend traditionally includes the best spices that a shopkeeper has on sale.

Five ways with beetroots

336

Make a statement

Make a shocking-pink risotto, a ruby-red borscht, or team them with soft, white goat's cheese in a green salad. Golden and striped varieties are available and these look great very thinly sliced and drizzled with balsamic syrup and fresh green herbs.

337

Roast it

When roasting, leave the skin on until the beetroot is cooked – the skin will then rub off easily, and it stops the colour of the beetroot from bleeding into any other vegetables. Depending on their size, beetroots need a long time in the oven – 60 to 90 minutes at 200°C.

338

Crunchy crisps

Make your own vegetable crisps by deep-frying very thinly sliced beetroots, parsnips, and sweet potatoes in small batches. Cook the beetroots last, if you don't want all your crisps to be pink! Drain on kitchen towel and sprinkle with sea salt and black pepper.

339

Grate it

Using a zester, julienne peeler or potato peeler, you can create fine strips of raw beetroots and carrots that look beautiful in a green salad.

340

Juice

Beetroot juice is super healthy and adds great colour to a drink. Try combining it with apple or grape juice for sweetness, or with orange or grapefruit to contrast the earthiness of the beetroot.

341 Winter vegetable hotpot

Makes 4

Ingredients

- 450 g swede
- 1 small turnip
- 2 carrots
- 1 large onion
- 115 g button mushrooms
- 225 g tomatoes
- 1 tablespoon miso paste
- 600 ml vegetable stock
- ½ teaspoon cayenne pepper
- ½ teaspoon ground cinnamon

Preparation

Preheat the oven to 180°C.

Peel the swede, turnip, carrots and onion, and slice them all thinly. Wipe the mushrooms. Peel and chop the tomatoes (see tip below).

Put all the vegetables into a casserole dish. Mix the miso paste with a little warm stock, then pour it into the dish and stir in the spices. Cover and bake for 90 minutes.

To peel tomatoes, prick the skins with a sharp knife and put them into a heatproof bowl. Cover them with boiling water and leave for a few minutes – the skins should start to split. Pour off the hot water and cover the tomatoes with cold water. The skins should loosen up and slide off easily. Don't leave the tomatoes in the boiling water too long as they will start to cook!

342 Fennel with ginger and orange sauce

Makes 4

Ingredients

- 1 large head fennel
- 1 clove garlic
- 2.5 cm ginger root
- 4 spring onions
- 2 tablespoons vegetable oil
- 1 orange
- 1 teaspoon soy sauce

Preparation

Cut the fennel into quarters and steam it for up to 10 minutes, until just tender. Peel and crush the garlic, grate the ginger and trim and chop the spring onions. Zest and juice the orange.

Warm the oil in a frying pan and gently cook the spring onions for three minutes, until soft. Stir in the garlic and ginger. Cook for a further minute, then add the orange juice and zest and the soy sauce. Heat through and pour over the warm fennel to serve.

343 Stuffed cabbage leaves
Serves 4

Ingredients
- 140 g mixed wild and basmati rice
- 1 onion
- 4 cloves garlic
- 125 ml apple cider
- 100 g raisins
- 1 small head Savoy cabbage
- 600 ml vegetable stock

Preparation
Preheat the oven to 180°C.

Put the rice into a medium-sized saucepan, cover with water and bring to the boil. Reduce the heat to a bare simmer, cover and cook for 50 minutes, topping up the water if necessary until the wild rice is tender. Drain and leave to cool. Peel and finely chop the onion. Peel and crush the garlic. Put the apple cider into a small pan and gently fry the onion, garlic and raisins in it until the onion is soft. Stir the mixture into the rice and mix thoroughly.

Prepare a large saucepan of boiling water. Trim the stalk of the cabbage and pull off all the leaves that are large enough to stuff – there are likely to be 12 to 15. Drop the leaves into boiling water and leave for five minutes to soften. Drain, and stuff each one with a spoonful of the rice mixture. Working on a flat surface, smooth out a leaf, put the stuffing in the centre and fold up the sides – then roll up. You can trim away any thick stems that make rolling difficult. Pour a little stock into the bottom of a baking dish and arrange the cabbage rolls on top, making several layers if necessary. Pour the rest of the stock over the dish, cover with a lid or foil and bake for 30 minutes.

Deceptively simple to prepare and always admired, stuffed cabbage leaves can be filled with spiced rice and kept in the oven on a low heat until needed. They're best served with a colourful tomato or cranberry relish.

344 Sweet potato gratin

Serves 4

Ingredients
- 900 g sweet potatoes
- 1 onion
- 1 tablespoon olive oil
- Salt and freshly ground black pepper
- 55 g salted butter
- 2 tablespoons plain flour
- 300 ml milk
- 150 ml single cream
- ½ teaspoon ground nutmeg
- 25 g pecans
- 55 g soft breadcrumbs

Preparation
Preheat the oven to 190°C.

Peel the sweet potatoes, cut them into large pieces and cook in boiling water for 25 minutes, until tender. Peel and finely chop the onion. Warm the oil and gently fry the onion until it is soft and translucent.

Grease a baking dish. Slice the sweet potatoes thickly and arrange a layer in the bottom of the dish. Cover with half of the onions and season with salt and pepper. Add a second layer of sweet potatoes and a second layer of onions. Season once more.

Melt the butter in a medium-sized saucepan, stir in the flour and cook for a minute before beating in the milk and single cream. Bring to the boil, mix in the nutmeg and simmer for three minutes. Pour the sauce over the vegetables. Finely chop the pecans and sprinkle over the top of the dish with the breadcrumbs. Bake for 30 minutes, until golden and bubbling.

345 Celery gratin with white wine and walnuts

Serves 4

Ingredients

- 2 heads celery
- 1 onion
- 2 tablespoons olive oil
- 2 bay leaves
- 100 ml white wine
- 275 ml vegetable stock
- 100 ml double cream
- 55 g walnuts
- 25 g salted butter
- 100 g soft breadcrumbs
- 25 g vegetarian Parmesan-style cheese

Celery is not just for salads and soups – here, it's the 'hero' ingredient. Simmered with bay leaves, bubbled with wine, baked in cream and topped with crispy breadcrumbs … it's a celebration.

Preparation

Trim the celery and cut each stick into 5-cm pieces. Peel the onion and slice thinly. Warm the olive oil in a heavy-bottomed saucepan. Stir in the celery, onion and bay leaves, reduce the heat to minimum, cover and cook for 20 minutes, stirring occasionally. Stir in the wine and stock, turn the heat to high and cook for up to eight minutes to reduce the liquid by two-thirds. Stir in the cream and continue to cook on a high heat for five minutes until the sauce is quite thick.

Roughly chop the walnuts. Melt the butter in a pan, stir in the breadcrumbs and walnuts, then stir over a medium heat for five minutes until golden brown. Grate the cheese. Preheat the grill to high. Transfer the celery into a baking dish, remove the bay leaves and top with the breadcrumbs and cheese. Put under the hot grill for three minutes or so, until browned and crisp. Serve immediately.

346 Gnocchi with sage pesto

Serves 4

Ingredients

- 1 kg potatoes
- 1 medium egg
- Salt and freshly ground black pepper
- 300 g plain flour

For the pesto

- 70 g hazelnuts
- 70 g fresh spinach
- 2 cloves garlic
- 75 ml olive oil
- 10 fresh sage leaves
- ½ teaspoon ground nutmeg
- Salt and freshly ground black pepper

Preparation

Boil the potatoes in their skins until tender. Drain, leave to cool slightly, then peel away and discard the skins. Beat the egg. Mash the potatoes with the egg and seasoning. Transfer to a large mixing bowl and stir in two-thirds of the flour. Turn the mixture onto a floured work surface or board. Gently knead the dough, gradually bringing in the remaining flour. This should only take a minute or two – don't overwork the dough. Divide the dough into four pieces and gently roll each one into a sausage shape. Cut into 2.5-cm pieces and refrigerate on a floured tray until needed.

To make the pesto, toast the hazelnuts in a dry pan for two minutes, and leave to cool completely. Put the nuts in a food processor with the fresh spinach, garlic and half of the olive oil. Process to a rough paste, using the pulse function, and gradually adding the remaining oil. Add the sage leaves and nutmeg, and pulse to combine. Season with salt and pepper.

Bring a large saucepan of salted water to the boil. Drop the gnocchi into the water, working in small batches so that the temperature of the water does not fall. The gnocchi is cooked when it rises to the surface. Scoop it out with a slotted spoon and serve immediately with the sage pesto.

347 Chestnut and red wine casserole

Serves 4

Ingredients

- 2 parsnips
- 1 sweet potato
- 175 g shallots
- 1 medium aubergine
- 1 courgette
- 2 red peppers
- 2 leeks
- 175 g button mushrooms
- 3 tablespoons olive oil
- 225 g tomatoes
- 85 g cooked, peeled chestnuts
- 2 cloves garlic
- 750 ml passata
- 300 ml red wine
- 2 bay leaves
- ½ teaspoon cinnamon
- Salt and freshly ground black pepper

Preparation

Peel the parsnips, sweet potato and shallots, then chop them all into bite-sized pieces. Chop the aubergine, courgette and red peppers, slice the leeks and trim and wipe the mushrooms. Heat the olive oil in a large, heavy-bottomed saucepan and fry the parsnips and sweet potato gently for 10 minutes, until soft. Stir in the shallots, peppers, aubergine, courgette, leeks and mushrooms. Cover and cook for a further five minutes.

Chop the tomatoes, halve the chestnuts and peel and crush the garlic. Stir these and all the remaining ingredients into the pan. Cook gently, covered, for a further 15 minutes. Adjust the seasoning with salt and pepper to taste.

Five ways with chestnuts

348
Simply roasted
Preheat the oven to 200°C. Carefully cut a cross into the shiny outer skin of each chestnut. Spread them out in a roasting pan and roast for around 30 minutes, until they split open.

349
Savoury mixture
Chopped, cooked chestnuts or unsweetened chestnut purée can be used to make a nut loaf, or combined with cranberries in a seasonal stuffing mix. Or, try wrapping a chestnut mixture in puff pastry to make a nut roast en croûte.

350
Chestnut flour pancakes
Make a gluten-free batter using 115 g rice flour, 55 g chestnut flour, 2 teaspoons baking powder, ½ teaspoon bicarbonate of soda, 2 beaten eggs, 125 ml semi-skimmed milk and a pinch of salt. Stack with layers of spinach, beetroot and squash.

351
Soup
Chestnut soup can be made from a base of fried carrot, parsnip and celeriac. Add cooked chestnuts with vegetable stock and a generous splash of sherry. Season with nutmeg. Purée, and top with chestnut pieces and a swirl of sour cream.

352
Candied
Marrons glacés are chestnuts candied in syrup. Eat them like sweets, purée them or chop them over vanilla ice cream.

353 Scandinavian mulled wine

Serves 6

Ingredients

- 60 ml vodka
- 1 cinnamon stick
- 5 cloves
- 1 bottle fruity red wine
- 1 teaspoon ground cinnamon
- ½ teaspoon ground ginger
- 115 g brown sugar

Preparation

Put the vodka into a large saucepan with the cinnamon stick and cloves, bring to simmering point and then set aside for at least an hour. When your guests arrive, pour in the wine and add the ground cinnamon, ginger and sugar. Serve warm.

This Scandinavian-style mulled wine packs a punch! Traditionally, this is served with raisins, which are put into the bottom of the glasses before filling up. Leave some teaspoons next to the punch bowl so guests can spoon the fruit out and eat it once they've finished their drinks.

354 Cranberry fizz

Serves 4

Ingredients

- 475 ml sparkling apple juice
- 475 ml cranberry juice

Preparation

Mix the two juices together and serve over ice.

This is a welcoming cocktail at any holiday occasion. For an alcoholic version, add a splash of gin or vodka, or use sparkling apple cider or pear cider.

355 Spiced chai tea

Serves 4

Ingredients

- 2.5 cm ginger root
- 1 cinnamon stick
- 1 litre water
- ¾ teaspoon fennel seeds
- 3 cloves
- 6 cardamom pods
- 4 English breakfast teabags
- 125 ml milk
- Honey or sugar to taste

Preparation

Roughly chop the ginger and break
the cinnamon stick into short pieces.
In a small saucepan, bring the water
to the boil, add the spices and ginger
and simmer for 10 minutes. Put the
teabags into the pan and simmer for
another four minutes.

Warm the milk in a separate pan and
pour it into the tea. Heat the mixture
for a further two minutes, strain and
serve. Add honey or sugar to taste.

356 Chilli hot chocolate

Serves 4

Ingredients

- 1 red chilli
- 1.5 litres milk
- 200 g plain chocolate
- 200 ml single cream

Preparation

Slice the chilli in half lengthways and
de-seed. Put the milk into a pan and
add the chilli. Bring the mixture to
a simmer, then remove from the heat
and allow to infuse for 10 minutes.

Break the chocolate into pieces.
Reheat the milk, add the single cream
with the chocolate and continue to
warm the mixture until the chocolate
is completely melted. Remove the
chillies just before serving.

357 Chilli chocolate chestnut cake

Serves 10

Ingredients
- 4 medium eggs
- 140 g caster sugar
- 250 g dark chocolate
- 250 g unsalted butter
- 1 to 2 teaspoons chilli powder, to taste
- 250 g cooked chestnuts
- 275 ml milk
- 2 to 3 drops almond essence

Preparation
Preheat the oven to 170°C. Grease and line a 23-cm springform cake tin with baking parchment.

Separate the eggs into yolks and whites and put them into separate mixing bowls. Beat the yolks with the caster sugar. Roughly chop the chocolate and put it into a small saucepan with the butter. Gently melt the chocolate and butter together. Stir in the chilli powder and mix well to avoid any lumps. Leave to cool a little and then stir into the egg yolks and mix thoroughly.

Peel the chestnuts if they still have their outer skins on. Roughly chop and put them into a small saucepan with the milk. Bring to the boil, stir in the almond essence and leave to cool for a few minutes before transferring to a food processor. Process until smooth and add to the chocolate mixture, mixing well to prevent any pale streaks in the cake.

Beat the egg whites to soft peaks and gently fold them into the chocolate mixture. Spoon the mix into the prepared tin, smooth the top and bake for up to 45 minutes – it may still be a bit wobbly. Leave to cool before taking the cake out of the tin and slicing to serve.

Chilli and chocolate have become a well-loved combination, especially appropriate for colder months. Thoroughly puréed chestnuts add a subtle sweet flavour and a grainy texture similar to ground almonds.

358 Red velvet cupcakes

Makes 12

Ingredients

- 225 g cooked beetroot
- 90 ml rapeseed oil
- 2 tablespoons lemon juice
- 1 teaspoon vanilla essence
- 4 tablespoons water
- 175 g plain flour
- 200 g granulated sugar
- 3 tablespoons cocoa powder
- 1 teaspoon baking powder

Preparation

Preheat the oven to 190°C. Grease a 12-cup cupcake tin or line with paper cases.

Peel the beetroot, if necessary, and put it into a food processor with the oil, lemon juice, vanilla essence and water. Blend to a smooth purée. Put the flour into a large bowl and mix together with the sugar, cocoa powder and baking powder.

Stir the wet ingredients into the dry ingredients and mix to combine. Divide the mixture between the cases and bake for 20 minutes, until risen and cooked through. Leave the cupcakes to cool before decorating with your choice of extravagant icing or melted vegan chocolate!

Do not use beetroot preserved in vinegar for this recipe!

359 Mincemeat and banana muffins

Makes 12

Ingredients

- 1 ripe banana
- 4 tablespoons vegetarian mincemeat
- 1 medium egg
- 60 ml milk
- 60 ml rapeseed oil
- 125 g plain flour
- 2 teaspoons baking powder
- 3 tablespoons brown sugar

Preparation

Preheat the oven to 200°C. Grease a muffin tin or line with paper cases.

Mash the banana and mix with the mincemeat in a small bowl. Whisk the egg, milk and oil together and put the flour, baking powder and sugar into a large mixing bowl and stir together. Add the egg and milk mixture, then the banana and mincemeat. Stir until just blended – do not overmix, or your muffins will be too firm and springy.

Divide the mixture between the cases and bake for 30 minutes, until a skewer pushed into the centre comes out clean. Cool on a wire rack.

360 Easy vegan fudge

Makes about 50 pieces

Ingredients

- 700 g caster sugar
- 600 ml soya milk
- 115 g vegan margarine
- 2 teaspoons vanilla essence

Preparation

Line an 18-cm square tin with baking parchment. Half-fill your kitchen sink with cold water.

Put the sugar, soya milk and margarine into a large saucepan and heat gently to melt the margarine and dissolve the sugar. Bring to the boil and simmer until the temperature reaches 120°C on a sugar thermometer. If you don't have a sugar thermometer, prepare a small bowl of cold water. When the mixture is ready, a little of it dropped into the water will form a soft ball.

When this point is reached, quickly stir in the vanilla essence (or another flavouring of your choice), then carefully take the pan off the heat and put it into the cold water in the kitchen sink, to cool the mixture down quickly. Beat it with a wooden spoon until it becomes very thick, then pour it into the prepared tin, smooth the top and leave at room temperature to set. When it is firm, remove it from the tin and cut it into small pieces with a sharp knife.

Overlap the baking parchment so that it hangs over the sides of the tin – this makes it easy to lift the fudge out when it has set.

361 Fruity teabread
Serves 8

Ingredients
- 225 g mixed dried fruit
- 225 ml freshly made black tea
- 225 g self-raising flour
- 115 g brown sugar
- 1 medium egg
- 2 tablespoons orange marmalade

Preparation
Put the dried fruit in a bowl, pour the tea on top and leave overnight to soak. Preheat the oven to 180°C. Grease and line a 700-g loaf tin.

Sift the flour into a large bowl and stir in the sugar. Beat the egg and add it to the dry ingredients along with the marmalade, the soaked fruit and any remaining soaking liquid. Mix thoroughly. Spoon the mixture into the prepared tin, smooth the top and bake for one hour, until a skewer inserted into the cake comes out clean. Leave to cool in the tin for 10 minutes before turning onto a cooling rack. Leave to cool completely before slicing.

Teabreads are traditional English cakes made with mixed dried fruit soaked overnight in black tea. Dense and moist, they are best baked in loaf tins and served sliced and buttered.

362 Almond rice pudding
Serves 6

Ingredients
- 85 g pitted dates
- 200 g brown rice
- 950 ml almond or soya milk
- 1 teaspoon almond essence
- ½ teaspoon ground cinnamon
- 85 g raisins
- 70 g toasted flaked almonds

Preparation
Put the dates in a bowl and cover them with boiling water. Leave to soak for 15 minutes, then transfer the dates and water to a blender and blend until smooth. Put the rice and almond or soya milk into a large saucepan, bring to the boil, then reduce the heat and simmer gently, stirring occasionally, for 45 minutes until the rice is cooked. Stir in the puréed dates, almond essence, cinnamon, raisins and almonds.

363 Raspberry cranachan

Serves 4

Ingredients

- 5 tablespoons oatmeal
- 150 ml whipping cream
- 2 tablespoons clear honey
- 2 tablespoons whisky
- 150 ml crème fraîche
- 400 g fresh raspberries

Preparation

Preheat the grill and line the grill pan with kitchen foil. Spread the oatmeal evenly in the pan and grill for about three minutes stirring occasionally, until golden. Leave to cool completely. Beat the cream until thick and fold in the crème fraîche. Stir in the honey and whisky, and then mix in 4 tablespoons of the toasted oatmeal.

Put a few fresh raspberries in the base of four glass serving dishes, top with a little of the cream mixture and continue to layer the fruit and the cream, ending with a layer of cream in each dish and reserving a few raspberries for decoration. Sprinkle with the reserved toasted oatmeal and decorate with the remaining raspberries. Serve immediately.

Cranachan is a traditional Scottish dessert. The splash of whisky is essential – use Scotch if you can!

364 Peanut butter truffles

Makes 18-20

Ingredients

- 115 g dates
- 115 g walnuts
- 115 g icing sugar
- 225 g vegan peanut butter (smooth or crunchy)
- 115 g vegan plain chocolate, plus extra grated chocolate to decorate

Preparation

Finely chop the dates and walnuts. Mix them together with the icing sugar and peanut butter. Roll into truffle-sized balls and put on a baking tray lined with baking parchment. Chill for up to 20 minutes. Roughly chop the chocolate and melt it in a small heatproof bowl over a saucepan of hot water.

Using a toothpick, dip the truffles into the melted chocolate, carefully put on the baking parchment and sprinkle with a little grated chocolate. Return to the refrigerator until the chocolate has set firmly.

365 Sticky marmalade cake

Serves 8

Ingredients

- 175 g unsalted butter
- 175 g brown sugar
- 330 g orange marmalade
- 2 medium eggs
- 55 g chopped crystallised ginger
- 55g chopped dates
- 1 teaspoon ground ginger
- 1 teaspoon ground allspice
- 175 g self-raising flour

Preparation

Preheat the oven to 190°C. Grease and line a deep 23-cm cake tin.

Melt 55 g of the butter in a small pan and stir in 55 g of the sugar and 150 g of the marmalade. Heat and stir until syrupy and then pour into the cake tin.

Beat the remaining butter and sugar together, then beat in the eggs. Chop the ginger and dates. Mix the spices into the flour and fold into the wet ingredients along with the crystallised ginger and dates. Fold in the remaining marmalade. Pour the cake mixture into the cake tin and spread it out over the marmalade syrup. Bake for 75 minutes, until just set. Allow to sit for 10 minutes before inverting onto a serving dish.

If you plan to use a springform tin for this, take the precaution of lining the base with a piece of baking parchment that extends a little way up the sides of the pan, and put the pan onto a baking tray before putting it into the oven, as it may leak. Serve with custard – I like to stir a little whisky into mine!

Index

Page numbers marked in **bold** indicate 'Five Ways With' entries.

Acknowledgements

I'd like to thank Drew Smith for dreaming up the concept for the book, Clarissa Hyman for bringing Drew and I together, Silvia Langford for giving the project the green light and all the team at Elwin Street Productions for bringing it together. And my husband Gwilym Hughes for his patience.

For more information about the Vegetarian Society, please visit www.vegsoc.org

Suppliers

Farmer's markets are a great source for fresh, local and seasonal fruits and vegetables – look online to find one near you.

There are also many shops and websites around the UK that stock and deliver fresh vegetables and wholefoods.

Abel & Cole: delivery nationwide, www.abelandcole.co.uk

Farmaround: delivery nationwide, www.farmaround.co.uk

Planet Organic: stores and fresh delivery in London and dry goods delivery nationwide, www.planetorganic.com

Wholefoods: stores in London, Cheltenham and Glasgow and delivery to parts of London, www.wholefoodsmarket.com

Holland and Barrett: stores and delivery nationwide, www.hollandandbarrett.com

Unicorn Grocery: www.unicorn-grocery.coop

Suma wholefoods wholesalers: ordering available through food groups, www.suma.coop

Clearspring: available nationwide, www.clearspring.co.uk

Picture credits